T

Born eight years apart, yet remarkably similar in many ways, Grace Kelly's two gorgeous daughters have led lives glittering with nearly unimaginable riches, fame, and opportunity. Heirs to both Hollywood and European royalty, Caroline and Stephanie have become unique and fascinating women.

Now this candid, uncensored story provides the answers to the questions everyone asks about Grace's girls:

- *What was their real relationship with their legendary mother?*

- *What special pressures drove them both to rebellion?*

- *What are they really like . . . their coolly elegant mother or their domineering royal father?*

- *What movie stars and celebrities have been entangled in their shocking romances?*

- *What do they need from love . . . and why do they make the wrong choices?*

- *What lies in the future—career, family, or aimless lives?*

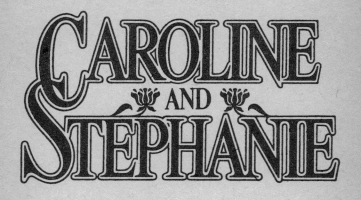

CAROLINE AND STEPHANIE

Susan Crimp and Patricia Burstein

ST. MARTIN'S PRESS/NEW YORK

CAROLINE AND STEPHANIE

Copyright © 1988 by Susan Crimp and Patricia Burstein

All rights reserved. No part of this book may be used or reproduced in any manner whatsoever without written permission except in the case of brief quotations embodied in critical articles or reviews. For information address St. Martin's Press, 175 Fifth Avenue, New York, N. Y. 10010.

Library of Congress Catalog Card Number: 87-63025

ISBN: 0-312-91116-5   Can. ISBN: 0-312-91117-3

Printed in the United States of America

First St. Martin's Press mass market edition/August 1988

10 9 8 7 6 5 4 3 2 1

Acknowledgments

The authors would like to thank the following people:

Princess Grace, Princess Caroline, and Princess Stephanie for making this story possible . . . Vera Maxwell, Father Peter Jacobs, Karen Hilton, Baron Christian de Massy, Professor Ray Browne, The Princess Grace Hospital, London, the Monaco Tourist Office, New York, Betsy Rosenfield Samet, our editor Charles Spicer and our family and friends in England and America.

Special thanks to Mr. F. Z. Crimp

Material for this book was gathered in personal interviews, and additional information was taken from the following sources:

The Daily Express, London
The Times, London
The New York Times
The New York Post
The New York Herald Tribune (now defunct)
United Press International
Time
Life
People
Gente, Italy
Cosmopolitan
The Washington Post
The Los Angeles Times
Vanity Fair
Tatler, England
Woman, England

BOOKS

Princess Grace by Sarah Bradford
Palace by Baron Christian de Massy and Charles Higham
Grace by James Spada

Contents

CONTENTS

PROLOGUE

Grace's Girls

IT is a world of privilege that most girls, who do not grow up to be princesses, can only imagine. In winter there was skiing in Gstaad, and in summer cruising or waterskiing along the Mediterranean coast or taking a luxurious dip in the private palace pool. The view from the 180-room pink palace that was their home opened to a blue-green sea where yachts swayed gently in the harbor. They draped themselves in Dior creations and other designer outfits, which, depending on their moods, they would alternate with blue jeans and casual sportswear. Lunches in the nearby city of Nice preceded dinners with the rich and famous. Then it might be off to Régine's nightclub to dance until near dawn.

But unlike many celebrities, who seek and eventually arrive at this gilded existence, Princesses Caroline and Stephanie of Monaco were born into it. A twenty-one-gun salute heralded the births, eight years apart, of both Caroline Louise Marguerite and Stephanie Marie Elisabeth. Between these years there was a boy, Albert Alexandre Louis Pierre, the only son and heir to the Principality of Monaco. Despite the royal significance attached to his birth, it would be the two daughters who would later claim the world's attention. Though his arrival was announced by the firing of 101 guns, it would be Grace's girls who eventually made the most noise.

On the face of it, there is no reason why Monaco, a principality smaller than New York's Central Park and whose only national industries seem to be tourism, gambling, and the sale of postage stamps, should be a constant media attraction. This French Riviera playground has been called everything from "a sunny place for shady people" to a "tin-pot principality" to "Las Vegas sur Mer." A tax haven for tycoons, Monaco has no apparent political or economic significance in the world. But it was not the gorgeous harbor with a backdrop of the French Alps or the international clientele or even its royal lineage that put Monaco on the map. Instead it was the Hollywood magic of American film star Grace Kelly. Her marriage on April 19, 1956, to Prince Rainier drew media from all over the world to the tiny principality.

The wedding was attended by 1,100 guests, including dignitaries from twenty-four countries, and 1,600 journalists. An estimated 30 million viewers saw the ceremony on television. Among the illustrious guests were ex-King Farouk of Egypt, Gloria Swanson, Ava Gardner, David Niven, the Aga Khan, and Aristotle Onassis. The Greek tycoon Onassis arranged for 15,000 carnations to be dropped on Rainier's yacht from a plane. The freshly washed stone cathedral was festooned with flowers; white lilies, lilacs, and hydrangeas illuminated by candles. The sun burned through a gray overcast to dominate the sky on the day of this union. Henceforth such a glorious day would be known as "Princess Grace Weather."

Ever since that day the press guard have refused to retreat. And they also caught up, at every turn, with her daughters.

With the death of Grace five years ago, the two princesses have had the limelight all to themselves. Of course, they never wanted it in the first place. Despite the relentless scrutiny of the world's media, the story of the two daughters has yet to be told. While striving to honor their mother's legacy, they also want to claim their own lives.

Pieces of Grace's personality can be found in all her children. While Albert reflects the shy and somewhat delicate parts of Grace, Caroline and Stephanie exhibit the more uninhibited, the exuberant side of their mother.

By the daughters' teens they were already in trouble. First there was Caroline losing all interest in school and devoting her time to gallivanting about discos and clubs. The Grimaldis considered sending her off to America—to Princeton University—for a more traditional campus life. That plan did not sit well with Caroline, who promptly fell in love with a man seventeen years her senior, and worse, a notorious playboy. As the romance grew and threatened to become a marriage, they tried to stall Caroline, to no avail. Wanting to avoid a royal rift, Grace and Prince Rainier decided to let her go ahead with it. Despite her doubts, Grace gave her daughter a wedding to remember, with some of the same splendor that had attended her own. Grace capitulated in large part to spare Caroline the agony she had suffered at the hands of her own parents, particularly her father, who all too often dampened her romantic yearnings. She could not have failed to notice that Caroline—

just like the young Grace Kelly—cottoned to an older man as a symbol of independence from family constraints. Grace would not make the same mistakes with her own children. But as fate would have it, Caroline, with Stephanie following in her footsteps, would make mistakes all on her own. Alas, it took her less than a year to wake up to the realization that her husband, Philippe Junot, was, in fact, a mistake. She sought and got a divorce. An annulment, which would redeem her in the eyes of the Catholic Church, eludes her to this day.

Just as it seemed Caroline was back on track, Stephanie, at sixteen, started stepping out of line. Once again, Grace was faced with a reluctant princess. "I hate being a princess," Stephanie, like her sister before her, was known to yell on several occasions. She acted out the part of royal rebel by getting thrown out of a strict Parisian Catholic school and turning up at discos and after-hours clubs with some unsuitable escorts. Not to mention photographers who caught her in various romantic embraces. Her wayward behavior came to an abrupt end with Grace's death in an automobile accident. Stephanie, at Grace's side in the car, has since been rumored to have been driving.

Following Grace's death, both daughters have taken facets of their mother's personality and adopted them as their own. Caroline, now married and the mother of three children, has taken on the royal responsibilities that belonged to her mother. Stephanie, on the other hand, still stretching her talents, has embarked upon a show business career, doing, in her own words, what her mother did in reverse: "My mother gave up stardom to be a princess. Now I'm giving up being a princess for stardom." Though she has already enjoyed professional success, in fashion and music, personally she has yet to get her act together. As the two princesses, one devoted to family and the other to career, perpetuate the legend of Princess Grace of Monaco, they are closer to becoming more whole human beings than scattered jet-setters.

Together, Princesses Caroline and Stephanie of Monaco bring to their respective roles Grace's elegance, exuberance, and, of course, her excellence.

CHAPTER 1

Little Princesses

THE birth of Princess Caroline was an event of epic Hollywood proportions. Church bells rang out. There was dancing in the streets. A twenty-one-gun salute boomed from two ancient cannon whistles on the palace rock where Rainier's ancestors had ruled for eight hundred years. Royal proclamations were on every billboard, previously covered with tourist posters of bathing beauties. The royal yacht, *Deo Juvante II*, and boats in the harbor were strung with covered lights and decked in pennants. *Deo Juvante II*, "With God's Help" (the prince's motto), was a wedding gift to Grace. *Deo Juvante II* had brought her to shore upon her arrival. Flags went up all over town. Champagne, provided free of charge by the palace, flowed freely.

The second-smallest country in Europe and the world, Monaco is 435 miles south-southeast of Paris and at the foot of the French Alpes-Maritimes and surrounded by the Riviera coastline. It is only a few miles west of the Italian border as well. With the country's 28,000 residents living on the one-mile square that comprises the principality, Monaco is also the most densely populated place in the world. Only about 4,000 people are native Monégasques; the rest represent 88 nationalities, attracted to Monaco's soft climate (mean year-round temperature, 62 degrees Fahrenheit) and tax status. There are four districts: Monaco-Ville, Old Monaco, which sits atop Le Rocher 200 feet above sea level and offers a unique view of the blue immensity of the Mediterranean; La Condamine, the port area; Fontvieille, an industrial area of La Condamine that was reclaimed by landfill in the 1960s and 1970s, and Monte Carlo, the site of the famed casino and tourist mecca. Palms, mimosa, and bougainvillea frame the old part of the city with its red-tiled roofs and winding cobblestone streets. The snappy red and white flags and the barber-pole sentry boxes of the 86-member palace guard lend a fairy-tale air to the place. The hodgepodge of condos and hotels in Monte Carlo is in sharp contrast to the older part. Despite the overdevelopment, this playground for the rich has probably changed very little from the nineteenth century when Russian princes tried their luck at the roulette tables. Today's "aristocrats" include not only moguls, but also writers (Harold Robbins and Anthony Burgess) and tennis stars (Boris Becker) and opera star Placido Domingo. Monaco for many remains a golden existence.

Enter Caroline Louise Marguerite, the thirty-first descendant of the Grimaldi warrior who claimed Monaco for his own in the twelfth century and heiress to twenty-four ancient European titles. The name Grimaldi is adopted from Grimaldo, the youngest son of Otto Canella who was consul of Genoa in 1133. The basically Genoese Grimaldis have ruled Monaco since the thirteenth century when Francisco Grimaldi, disguised as a monk, seized the citadel on the

rock. The Grimaldis owe their surviv
wars and revolutions, marriages to Eu
and the enmity between France and Ital
later intermarriages they became more Fr
Italian. The most recent threat to its so reignty
came in 1962 when then French President Charles
de Gaulle, angered by the large number of French
citizens—mostly from Algiers—settling there to
avoid French taxes, threatened to cut off French water and electrical supplies to the principality. French
guards, stationed at the border, checked passports.
After de Gaulle turned down Rainier's request for an
audience with him, the dispute was resolved by a
new Monégasque constitution that made it illegal for
French citizens who settled there after 1962 to avoid
French income taxes.

Caroline arrived at 9:27 A.M. (3:27 A.M., New York
time) on January 23, 1957. She weighed in at eight
pounds, three ounces. Prince Rainier went on the
radio to announce the birth to his 4,200 Monégasque
subjects, and in a call-in segment after described his
firstborn as "very beautiful, just lovely." A twenty-
six-year-old Princess Grace wept with joy and expressed a wish to nurse her baby. "I am very happy
indeed," she said, sipping champagne to toast her
firstborn. By then she had been married exactly nine
months and five days. The only slightly sour note
came from Grace's father back in Philadelphia. "Oh,
shucks," he was quoted as saying, "I wanted a boy."

A baby, no matter the gender, was just fine with
the locals as well as the tycoons and titled in residence. No longer would they have to worry, without
an heir, about being subject to France's high taxes
and military draft. A national holiday—except for
casino croupiers—was declared. In another outburst
of celebration Rainier granted a general amnesty for

all prisoners sent up on minor charges prior to Caroline's birth. This show of forgiveness was greeted, in part, by some reluctance from prisoners quite content to reside at the plush jail offering a splendid view of Monaco, food from local restaurants, and civilized guards. He also signed a state document forgiving all of Monaco's traffic offenders.

Almost from the moment of birth Caroline was a hot press property. Every detail of her day-old existence was chronicled in papers all over the world. This even included the weather report of heavy rains portending, in Riviera folklore, the likelihood of prosperity, health, and character to all children born under drenching skies. Though Grace agreed to present a trousseau to all babies born in Monaco that day, Caroline was the only one. One of the first palace bulletins on her birth described Caroline as having dark hair and a tiny frecklelike imperfection on her nose.

Her dual European-American upbringing was evident from the outset. While baby Caroline rested in the same gilded wood cradle in which her father had been rocked as a baby, she was weighed on an ordinary scale that came from her grandmother in Philadelphia. Rainier stated the baby was Monégasque and nothing else, but the U.S. Consul in Nice told him the baby had the right to American citizenship as well.

The baby's nurse, Maureen Stahl, was a compromise choice. Rainier wanted an English girl and Grace an American. They settled on the Swiss Stahl who immediately took command and would address the baby princess as "Madame." The Irish-American Grace recommended a less royal approach to childrearing. The little "Madame," she said amusedly, would be spanked whenever she deserved it. But so far, so good—Caroline, nursed and bottle-fed, slept solidly between 9:30 P.M. and 6 A.M. at her mother's bedside. Grace later joined La Leche League, which advocates breast-feeding, solely on the basis of her maternal instinct. "Wholly normal and right," she said. "I never considered doing anything else."

Two days after her birth Caroline was officially registered as heiress-presumptive to the throne of Monaco. This would be, as it turned out, her first royal protest. As Prince Rainier certified the infant before a judge and three witnesses, and then had her name inscribed in the Grimaldi archives, Caroline responded by howling and chewing her fists.

Only a brother could bail her out of this situation. Otherwise Caroline would one day rule Monaco. Contrary to general thinking, a Monégasque prince's heir need not be male. Further, nothing in Monaco's Constitution—the last one promulgated in 1962— makes it illegal to name Caroline heir to the throne. Ironically, though, women only got the right to vote for the National Council, the highest government body, that same year, and participated for the first time in the 1963 elections. Princess Grace, as it turned out, was largely responsible for women's enfranchisement in Monaco. It was only in 1945 that women were allowed to even vote in municipal elections.

Already the press was courting her and offered large sums of money, in dollars, francs, marks, pesetas, and lire, for exclusive photos of the infant princess. Rainier decided, through his American publicist, to sell to the highest bidders. The monies would go to the Monaco Red Cross, which would become a favorite charity of Grace's throughout her life. Most of the photography was done by Howell Conant, Grace's friend, for $1,000 per week plus expenses, a nominal sum in today's marketplace where $10,000 would be more like it.

Daily newspaper and wire-service photographers virtually stormed the palace gates and came away with pooled shots of mother and child. *Look* got the first four weeks of exclusive pictures and *Life* the first visit to the palace. *Jours de France* won the bidding over *Paris Match*. This was a blow to the latter, whose editor had arranged the photo session that brought Caroline's parents together while Grace was still a film star and Rainier a bachelor looking for a suitable wife to give him an heir.

The magazine's movie editor, Pierre Galante, was trying to find a photo feature at the 1955 Cannes Film Festival that would thoroughly captivate his readers. American actress Grace Kelly, who had just won an Oscar for *The Country Girl* and whose tantalizing role with Cary Grant in *To Catch a Thief* would be shown at the festival, fit the bill. *Paris Match*'s managing editor then mused aloud about asking Grace to pose with Prince Rainier. Instantly, they saw headlines: "Prince Charming Meets Movie Queen." Once Galante, through a mutual friend, was able to meet Grace and convince her, feelers were put out to the prince. The meeting itself almost fell apart. First, the car in which Grace was being driven was hit in the back by the car carrying the *Paris Match* photographers. But there was no damage per se. Then, the prince was late. Still, he managed to charm Grace with a tour of his gardens and private zoo. Grace was particularly impressed by how the prince put his arm inside a cage to pet one of his lions.

Even then, Prince Rainier seemed paranoid about the press. As his nephew, Baron Christian de Massy, eight years older than the princess, remembers:

"When we were allowed to visit her bedroom after a week and saw Grace with Caroline in her arms, I brought with me a Kodak Brownie camera and took shots of the radiant mother and child. As we left, overjoyed at the big occasion, the official palace photographer asked me politely for my roll of film. By royal order it would have to be developed in the palace darkroom and not in a commercial photography shop." This move would be the start of a palace policy to control publicity about the two princesses. Later on, when the princesses were grown up, the palace would even buy negatives of them that might damage the royal image. From time to time, Rainier, who threw up his hands despairingly and declared, "I really would shoot these people if I had my way," had some offending journalists detained by the police. Attempts by his bodyguards to block paparazzi proved largely useless—telephoto lenses made this impossible. On one occasion, though, an Italian editor of a tabloid was thrown in jail for about two weeks for publishing faked nude photos of Caroline.

Caroline, meanwhile, was developing an aversion to the camera. "She has a prejudice against her father's camera," Grace wrote in a bylined article that appeared in *The New York Herald Tribune.* "When he wants to photograph her, which is often, he must do it surreptitiously."

Already, too, Grace had found some distortions in the coverage of her baby daughter's life. "No, little Caroline does not suck her thumb; not yet anyway," she stated emphatically. "She certainly does not suck all her fingers as some monster suggested." Grace also observed in the same article: "As she gets older —she is five-and-half weeks this weekend—I think she looks more and more like the Prince, particularly the upper part of her face. She has dark blue eyes like

Rainier, much darker than mine, and his broad forehead. Her mouth is said to be like mine. She has a lovely complexion, absolutely without blemish, and light brown hair."

Caroline's christening was a beautiful tableau as much as a photo opportunity. The day before, two thousand guests gathered in the Palace Court of Honor. Grace, standing at the top of a marble stairway, held a rose-bordered white wool blanket out of which Caroline's tiny face peered at admirers. Four bishops and fifteen priests officiated at the christening. Inside the Cathedral of Monaco, decked with ten thousand branches of white lilacs and tulips, the Most Reverend Gilles Barthe pronounced, "Caroline Louise Marguerite, I baptize you in the name of the Father and the Son and the Holy Ghost," before a thousand guests. Caroline started to squall in the arms of her godmother, Margaret Davis of Philadelphia, the ten-year-old niece of Princess Grace. The godfather, seventeen-year-old Prince George Festetics, stood by holding Caroline's hand. Caroline, whose weight would be monitored by the press throughout her teen and adult years, was reported then to have gained one pound, thirteen ounces. The baby princess wore the same dress, trimmed with Valenciennes lace, as both Rainier and his sister, Antoinette, did at their baptisms back in the twenties. Monégasques celebrated with fireworks in the streets. They also sent Chinese vases, a hobby horse, parakeets in a gilded cage, and a silver baby service to the infant princess.

From the palace balcony, Rainier, in the uniform of the Colonel of the Carabiniers, and Grace, in a beige mink coat, held up Caroline for the Monégasques who gathered in the square to get a glimpse of the woman who might one day rule over them.

Caroline's nursery, made out of a palace store-room, was a small suite next to the private apartments. There were two bedrooms, a playroom, and a kitchen with a refrigerator. All the rooms overlooked the Mediterranean. The nursery was crammed with nearly one hundred toys, including a vast array of stuffed animals, poodles and sheep among them. A birds-and-rabbit wallpaper design complemented the infant princess's stuffed-animal collection. Presiding over the nursery staff was Ann Wainstall, who had come from England thirty years before to attend Prince Rainier's sister. As did her cradle and christening gown, Caroline's nursery also had tradition. Unbeknownst to Caroline, playing in her nursery, over one hundred fan letters poured into the palace daily.

At ten months, she appeared with her parents on the balcony to review the parade honoring Rainier's eight years of rule. On the occasion of her first birthday, the palace issued a communiqué: "She now has six teeth and she weighs '10 kilograms, 300 grams' [roughly 22 pounds]. She is a superb child, laughing and gay, who loves to enjoy herself and is very sociable."

Not long after Caroline's birth Grace hoped aloud that her second child would be a son to spare Caroline the public life demanded of an heiress to the throne. That way, in Grace's words, Caroline could "grow up to be anything she likes—even an actress."

That wish came true when Albert Alexandre Louis Pierre, weighing in at eight pounds, eleven ounces, arrived on the palace scene on March 14, 1958. A 101-gun salute heralded his birth. Only fourteen months into her reign as heiress-presumptive, Caroline lost her position as Serene Highness. Now playing second fiddle to the tiny, chestnut-haired prince, she was taught to curtsy by her father before her day-old brother. The first hint of any sibling rivalry may have occurred at the official presentation of her baby brother to Monégasques the day before his baptism. Caroline interrupted a speech then by the mayor of Monaco with an "Ah!" into the microphone. Then, with a rebelliousness she displayed in her late teens, she took a sip from her father's glass when he wasn't looking. As the male offspring of Prince Rainier, Albert became heir apparent, preceding her in all rights of inheritance.

From now on the Armed Forces and the Fire Brigade would salute Prince Albert. Next to Albert's royal prerogatives, Caroline's privileges seemed plebian. She only got free seats at the movies and permission to get on railroad platforms without a ticket. Her baby brother would have a complete run of his father's royal boxes at theaters and football games, and he could sing in the choir. They both had equal billing at the Monte Carlo Casino—during their lifetimes neither of them could ever enter. Before the birth of Caroline, the royal couple apparently bet on a boy as their firstborn. According to published reports, the baby clothes they ordered prior to Caroline's birth from the Charles James salon in London were designed for a boy. The wardrobe included boxer shorts and little pants with side-buttoned "dentist coats" to match, as well as a cashmere opera cape with a white piqué collar. A last-minute adjustment produced clothes more suitable for a little princess. Fortunately, Mr. James had the goods in stock—simple designs he had introduced after the birth of his own child. Some of her clothes, with a minimum of frills, were specially cut, and others were available in stores.

With the pressure to produce a male heir to the

principality behind her, the birth of a third child, Princess Stephanie Marie Elisabeth de Grimaldi, was a more relaxed affair. Caroline and Albert listened for the number of cannon blasts to determine whether they had a new brother or sister. Like her brother and sister, Stephanie was born in the palace. She weighed six pounds, ten ounces. Her arrival on February 1, 1965, was announced by a twenty-one-gun salute.

To Grace, Stephanie was a gift from heaven. Still bereaved over her father's death five years before, in 1960, and recovering from two miscarriages, Grace had longed for this third child. With the older children now engaged in school and sports, any creative twitches the former Grace Kelly had about resuming some film work were deflected by her joy over her new baby. Grace had been offered the lead in Hitchcock's *Marnie*. Though the prince agreed to let her return briefly to a movie role, to be filmed during the family's holiday period, the Monégasques vetoed this option. The timing could not have been worse. This was in 1962, when Rainier was locked in battle, so to speak, with de Gaulle's French government. How would Monégasques perceive their princess, a rallying point during the crisis, if she played a sexually repressed Marnie, a criminal who is raped in the film? What about the screen kisses? No—the local citizenry wanted Grace to play the part of the Princess of Monaco, not Marnie. They made their objections known quite vocally. Another, though lesser, argument against resuming her film career had to do with the probability of a legal battle between MGM, to whom Grace was under contract, and Hitchcock, who argued that her seven-year agreement had ended with the studio. Not so, MGM countered, on the theory that once Grace resumed her career, the contract still stood. In the face of her subjects' outcry and an impending legal battle, Grace surrendered her dream of ever returning to the silver screen.

If Stephanie did not grab as many headlines as her siblings did at birth or inspire a collective sigh of relief from Monégasques about no taxes or a military draft, she received an outpouring of affection inside the palace gates. As the baby in the family, she was doted on and pampered. "This is the happiest day of my life," Caroline squealed with delight upon seeing her baby sister for the first time.

Despite Albert's initial apprehension, voiced by the request "Can it be a boy next time?" she would become his closest ally on the homefront. As it turned out, there would be no next time. As such, Grace and Rainier were clearly going to get as much enjoyment as possible from what they felt God had bestowed upon them. By the time Stephanie came along, her mother was already comfortable with her role as a European princess. Caroline, on the other hand, was born only nine months after the marriage, while Grace was still adapting to her own life abroad. As Rainier reflected upon their tenth anniversary: "It was more than moving from an American life to a European life and from a single to a married life. Most women doing that have at least the privacy of their homes. But she did not even have this. She had a palace but no home of her own." On top of pleasing the Monégasques, who clearly would have preferred a European aristocrat to an American actress as their princess, she gave birth to two children in the space of two years.

Much like any normal mother, one of her concerns was finding more space for the family's latest addition. Stephanie arrived, as did Caroline, a few days earlier than expected. A wing of the palace, destroyed during the French Revolution, was rebuilt to accommodate her.

On a cold Saturday in March, on the forty-first day of her life, Princess Stephanie was christened in Monaco's cathedral, adorned with lilacs, lilies, tulips, and white roses. Stephanie gave out a little cry as she was baptized. Then, in a centuries-old tradition, she was presented to Monégasques gathered, as they did before for Caroline and Albert, in the palace courtyard. From the flower-decked balcony, Prince Rainier told his subjects, "She comes to us in all her innocence and purity, bringing us more joy and happiness, as did her brother and sister . . . and yes, indeed, pride, for she like them is the symbol and base of a family and patriotic union of which we can justly be proud."

Princess Stephanie, cradled in her mother's arms, was a most serene princess. But the moment anyone else tried to hold her, Stephanie started wailing. Once nestled against Grace again, the baby princess quieted down and became quite calm. This bonding between mother and daughter would grow and endure over the years. Ironically, Stephanie would be at her mother's side at the end.

Both daughters, Grace noted, were born under the sign of Aquarius. Just after Stephanie's birth, Grace told a friend, "The water bearer is not a good sign for little princesses. It's too unpredictable, terribly perverse. She's going to be a handful, I'm afraid."

CHAPTER 2

Growing Up Royal

GROWING up for any girl is difficult. But for a princess it can be even more problematic. Living in a magic castle with the Mediterranean virtually at their front door and international celebrities gracing their dining table, the two princesses led lives that seemed like fairy tales.

Yet nannies, private teachers, guards, and bodyguards could not shield them from the pains attendant to privilege. Something as ordinary as a report card or a teenage crush, normally a private matter, would become an international headline. Whereas most children have clearly defined roots, the Princesses of Monaco dwelt in two different cultures, if not centuries. Their duty to abide by ancient European traditions was matched only by their appetite for all things American. They spoke English to their mother and French to their father.

They would grow up not only rich and beautiful, but also royal. Not even the world's most famous women, Jackie Onassis or Liz Taylor, could lay claim to this. The title of princess held a certain magic in a weary world. Fame was also bestowed upon them by virtue of their Oscar-winning movie-star mother, Grace Kelly, who gave up Hollywood to marry a prince. Throughout her life, the Philadelphia-born Grace Kelly would try to bring normality to her daughters' gilded lives.

That would not be an easy proposition. The princesses grew up in a 180-room castle. The family's ornate living quarters were a mixture of French Empire and Italian Baroque. They woke up to soft, fresh mornings, with the narrow medieval streets already washed and a profusion of flowers lacing the air with pleasant fragrances. From the palace they had a view of the Mediterranean and the French Alps. Nights they could watch the lights from yachts in the harbor twinkle and the moon make silver ripples in the sea. The "serenades" in the palace courtyard were hardly mariachi bands, but more like the Monte Carlo Philharmonic Orchestra.

Other nights they might attend a pop concert at the Monte Carlo Sporting Club where the likes of Harry Belafonte, Gilbert Bécaud, or Al Jarreau would be appearing in the Salles des Etoiles. While they were young they would go to sleep before night fell, but in their late teens it would sometimes be as dawn was spreading itself over the principality. Usually they would be emerging from one of the local clubs or discos.

Monaco was as much a playground as a palace. As the brochures describe the area: "Beside the Mediterranean, sparkling under the Riviera sun, the focus is on sport and leisure, golf, tennis, squash, sightseeing helicopter flights, water sports of all kinds . . . the opportunities are many and varied." And, of course, there is the lure of the roulette wheel.

No one ever broke the bank at the casino, but

many destroyed their marriages and reputations on the tables there. Edward the Seventh, Prince of Wales, was attracted to the local women as much as to the casino and scandalized Queen Victoria with a series of affairs. The queen had the curtains drawn on her train so she need not look on "that awful place." For a period of his retirement Winston Churchill lived at the Hotel de Paris. Nights he would hobble over to the roulette tables and sit there chomping on an unlit cigar, sipping 1918 Napoleon brandy. Playing the numbers 18 and 22 brought him luck. This was hardly the expected posture of one of Britain's and the world's greatest statesmen.

Both princesses were natural athletes. At five Caroline was a crack swimmer, with a faultless breast- and backstroke. Stephanie, the undisputed tomboy of the family, was swimming the entire length of the palace pool by the age of two. Because of her love of water she was known as the "little fish." Stephanie, inspired by Olga Korbut, the tiny (four feet eleven inches, eighty-four pounds) Russian gymnast who won three gold medals and one silver medal at the 1972 Olympic games in Munich, West Germany, also developed an insatiable appetite for gymnastics. They also waterskied, went motorboating and sailing, took horseback riding lessons, and played tennis. Winters they learned to ski at the family's rented chalet in Gstaad.

The palace provided plenty of amusement for the children. There was the prince's zoo, the one he showed Grace the very first time they met. Caroline had her own lion. At six she was petting a tame chee-tah. Of his palace zoo, Rainier once remarked: "Most of them are very friendly and have become pets of the family." Both princesses would develop an affec-tion for animals. Stephanie, at twenty, would take her German shepherd puppy, Atmo, to meetings; Caroline would, at eighteen, pose for a portrait with her Yorkshire terrier, Tiffany.

Along with the zoo creatures there were stuffed animals and other pleasures. "They had everything," Caroline's childhood friend Hélène Faggionato remembers. "Play kitchens that cooked. Play cars that drove, live animals and stuffed animals and everything." At six Caroline received a power-motored miniature car from Onassis, the Greek shipping tycoon, before he fell out with the prince.

Onassis would be forced to relinquish his controlling interest in the Société des Bains de Mer to Rainier. A remark by Onassis that his two favorite "playthings" were his yacht and the SBM caused the prince great concern. To Rainier, the Société was crucial to the future development of Monaco. Thus the Greek tycoon's attitude seemed far too flippant and self-involved for Rainier's tastes. Onassis even spoke a heresy—he suggested that gambling be abolished in Monte Carlo because it was immoral. By the early sixties, too, Onassis cruised in and out of Monte Carlo; although less than before, in part because of memories of a beloved wife who left him. By 1966 Rainier, foreseeing an ugly public battle, devised a plan whereby Onassis's control of the SBM would be diluted by issuing six hundred thousand additional shares in the corporation. Monaco would buy up the shares, and thus hold controlling interest. Onassis took the matter to the Monaco Supreme Court, but lost his case. By then a less combative Onassis, getting on in years and spending much of his energy courting Jacqueline Kennedy, gave in to Rainier's plan, but sold all his shares in the SBM at a profit of nearly 1,000 percent. Whatever the price, Rainier was at last in full command of Monaco's future. As such, the prince had the biggest piece of action in the principality. The Société owns the casino, hotels, the opera, restaurants, nightclubs, the sporting club, the tennis courts, the golf course, and three major swimming areas. In short, the princesses' daddy was close to becoming an absolute mogul as much as monarch. By the age of two Caroline had already met the future queen of Spain, Sophia, and at three, Charles de Gaulle. With the former, Caroline would show some of her future willfulness. She was supposed to present the future queen with a small bouquet, but instead refused to hand it over and teased her with it. At six, while on a state visit to Ireland, Caroline observed crowds fussing over Winston Churchill. "Is he more important than my daddy?" the princess asked her nanny.

Though royalty, the princesses were as subject as commoners to the ordinary rules of mortal families. In this family's hierarchy, Caroline took the firstborn's role of bossy older sister; Stephanie, the pampered youngest child; and Albert the somewhat discomfited middle child. As in most families, they formed varying alliances to suit their own purposes. Often Albert and Stephanie teamed up against Caroline, whose great passion from age fourteen on, according to a palace aide, was "to act sophisticated and older than her years." "We both used to gang up against Caroline," says Stephanie, "because she always treated me like a kid sister."

Stephanie and her brother, whom she referred to as "my sweetheart," often played together as children. "We would organize weddings," Stephanie remembers, "between my Barbie Doll and his Action Man." Caroline also had some gripes. "Albert and I couldn't watch television on school nights," she recalls. "But that didn't apply to Stephanie. I guess parents mellow about the time the third child rolls around." Unlike her older siblings, Stephanie did not have to straighten up her room.

A greater sense of duty and responsibility belonged to Caroline in her position as firstborn. Even at fifteen she could be counted on to keep a secret. A cousin, Christian de Massy, eight years her senior, consulted her about a motor-racing career. "I went to Caroline to discuss motor-racing and get her advice," he says. "I asked her not to say anything to the prince. And though I expected her to, she didn't." Caroline also helped her younger siblings with their homework and other problems. A close family friend, Vera Maxwell, once the preeminent fashion designer of her day, views the children in a most interesting way. "Caroline was the mother," she explains. "Stephanie was the tomboy. Albert was caught between the two sisters. He stuttered and was so self-conscious. I think he suffered from not pleasing his father, who wanted him to be a great sailor, which he is now, but wasn't then. It's too bad Albert didn't have Stephanie's character and vice versa."

Albert, with his blond, delicate, and shy nature, evoked memories of Grace as the most fragile member of the Kelly clan. Stephanie was more a throwback to the Kelly athletes, a tomboy who was always in jeans. Caroline, with her deep-set dark blue eyes, resembled the Mediterranean Grimaldis—especially her paternal grandmother Princess Charlotte—more than the Philadelphia Kellys in both appearance and spirit. "Rainier doted on the girls," Maxwell says. "He could be strict with Albert, who was docile."

Nor would the children be immune to the normal friction between parents over bringing them up. Asked in a 1982 *People* interview several months before her death if she and Rainier agreed as parents,

Grace responded: "My husband is a good father concerned about his children. His parents were divorced when he was young, so family life has a special meaning for him. On basics, on principles, we are very much agreed. Like many fathers, though, he sometimes is too strict and sometimes too lenient. I have been more in touch with the children for everyday problems and questions of discipline. It's not always the choice, but somebody has to do it."

A normal childhood, to Grace's thinking, would reflect her own strict Catholic upbringing in Philadelphia. "I tried to give them what were the good qualities of American youth," Grace said, "and to instill the same qualities our parents gave us." To this end both princesses attended summer camp in the Poconos for a few seasons with their Philadelphia cousins. Grace and her mother had also gone there. There they picked up slang like "guys" and "kids," and Caroline learned to stick her index finger in her mouth and whistle through her teeth. Of course, their bunkmates asked if they called their father "Your Royal Highness."

Normally the children would visit the United States for a month to six weeks each year. When the time came, they also made a traditional American tour of colleges—Williams and Amherst—with Albert. Then they took a private vacation on Lake Winnipesaukee in New Hampshire and also spent three days on Nantucket south of Cape Cod. Caroline was eighteen and Stephanie ten at the time. The following year the princesses and their parents visited Jackson Hole, Wyoming, and Santa Fe, New Mexico. In Wyoming they went river-rafting and in New Mexico saw the Indian culture. They stayed at a luxury resort near the Pueblo Indian community. At night they attended the Santa Fe Opera and dined with the governor of the state and his wife. At the age of two Stephanie, in her mother's arms, met Fred Astaire on the Warner Brothers set of *Finian's Rainbow* while Rainier went off to Disneyland with Caroline and Albert.

The Grimaldis always tried to take their children along wherever they went. One night, however, when their parents went alone to the wedding of Greece's then King Constantine, Caroline and Albert were so disappointed that their nanny held a dress ball of their own in the nursery. Caroline wore a long lace gown and Albert the dress uniform of an American Marine. Later little Stephanie would cling to her mother's skirts or refuse to let go of her hand. And Grace felt guilty whenever she left the principality. "I want to be in charge of my children," Grace insisted. To this end she found an English nanny named Maureen King who was not too fierce or old-fashioned in her ways to lock Grace out of her children's lives. The princess did not find the governess through traditional means. A letter arrived from King's sister, recommending her, while Grace was expecting Albert. Three months after his birth, King started work there.

King remembers the interview. Pinned against the wall by a huge Rhodesian Ridgeback dog, she then had to speak French in the interview with Rainier. "One felt," King observed, "that they didn't want a standard nurse in charge." Notwithstanding the nanny's presence, Grace and Rainier were determined to spend as much time with their children as possible. They all had breakfast together and, whenever possible, lunch. Grace read the princesses bedtime stories. "Mum used to cry reading Lassie to us as kids," Caroline recalled. If the prince was too busy to say good night in person, they rang him in the palace study.

While the two older children were supervised by King, Stephanie had several governesses. "Unfortunately for her," Maxwell recalls, "she had a very impersonal governess who was more interested in her boyfriend. Before that one there was one who was even worse." Of the older children's nanny, King, Maxwell remarks, "Marvelous. She had a wonderful way with them. Her psychology was incredible. She would tell them, 'Now, if you're good, you can have a piece of cheese,' as if it were chocolate."

Of the three children, it was Stephanie who was most in need of discipline. As the baby in the family, she was excessively pampered. She was inseparable from her mother and sucked her thumb in public. "She was sulking and being pissed off all the time," a cousin remembers. "She was always holding on to her mother's skirts. She would walk in holding her mother's dress much past the age one normally does that." Gwen Roberts, a friend and biographer of Grace, wrote: "Stephanie was iron-willed from the cradle—capable of great sweetness and naturalness too, but that wild streak in her was never far from the surface!" She was a tomboy always in motion. By the age of six she was confident on skis. She often accompanied her father to Monaco football games. A former nanny remembers: "She was inclined to rush off at a tangent, relying on her personality rather than her title to carry a thing through, right or wrong."

Just like any caring parents, with more than adequate resources, the Grimaldis gave their little princesses ballet, swimming, tennis, horseback riding, piano and flute lessons. Grace would stop by the Marika Besdrasova Ballet School to check on their progress. At thirteen Caroline showed a cool and graceful manner while Stephanie, at five a beginner, struggled with her jetés. Though Caroline starred, at eight, as one of the three kings in a children's play and, at eleven, in the play *Puss in Boots*, she left things at that. "Acting—absolutely never!" Caroline would declare years later. "Then I'd be compared to my mom." Playing the part of princess proved at times equally unappealing. In her early teens, Caroline was stopped in a store by a matron who said, "You look like Princess Caroline." To which she replied: "No, I don't—I look like Ali McGraw." At different times, both Caroline and Stephanie would complain, "I hate being a princess."

There were also Girl Scouts, pajama parties, and picnics with other girls from the local Catholic girls' school, which Caroline attended from age seven. Previously, she was privately tutored at the palace. Later Caroline would say that she did not need many friends because she had learned how to be alone. The only difference between the princesses and the other girls on outings was the presence of a guardian following them. One of Caroline's games, according to a friend, was to lose him. When school chums came to visit, they would observe the Palace Guard saluting Caroline and Stephanie.

As the princesses grew up, there would ultimately be no escape from the press. At eleven, Caroline had her first encounter with notoriety when a rock disc jockey in Monaco named his show *Radio Caroline*. At thirteen, still looking like a child with long straight hair parted in the middle, she was photographed in a bikini. "There is freedom of the press," Grace once said, "but not much freedom from it." When it wasn't possible to hide from photographers Stephanie stuck her tongue out at them.

One of the worst violations, said Father Peter Jacobs, an activist New York City priest and family friend, took place in December 1963, after the assassination of President Kennedy. As Grace would do throughout their childhoods, she took the princesses to the annual Monte Carlo Circus Festival. "They came to one of those booths where you throw baseballs and knock over things," he remembers Grace telling him. "And Gracie took the rifle and shot it. A photographer took a shot of Grace with the rifle and then juxtaposed it with the rifle used to kill Kennedy. What the paper was trying to say was that an Irish President had been assassinated in the States, and here was Grace Kelly, with her Philadelphia Irish origins, playing with a rifle at the same time. The children were also in the photo. This was an example, Grace said, of how the press hurt her and her children." Worse, the photo appeared in a respectable newspaper in Grace's native Philadelphia.

They lived at the palace during the week and spent many weekends and summer months at Roc Agel, an old farmhouse on a green ledge high up on the slopes of Mont Agel above Monaco. Prince Rainier had bought the sixty-acre property in 1959. Under Grace's supervision, the old house was transformed and enlarged without losing its original character. The place, with its brown tiled roof, massive beams, stone walls, and exquisitely carved woodwork, was a precious refuge for the Grimaldi family. As far as they were concerned, it was sacred—strictly for family and a few very close friends.

Local folks called Roc Agel "the ranch." There was American plumbing. The kitchen was done in Grace's favorite color, aquamarine. There were Rainier's horses and the children's ponies, as well as goats, cows, and rabbits. Grace also had a swimming pool installed to give the children an added facility. An Italian couple looked after the house. But on weekends Grace liked to do the cooking. She experimented with Chinese and Italian dishes. The prince also worked the land on a tractor. There were also barbecues with the prince in the role of chef. At her grandmother Charlotte's château outside Paris, Caroline started riding and hunting—pheasants and partridge usually—from the time she was twelve.

Princess Caroline was always wanting to meet Caroline Kennedy. At the age of eight, they had a playdate in New York's Central Park. The troll doll she received for her tenth birthday from the President's daughter would be her favorite present that year. Grace would later follow Jackie Kennedy's lead by allowing a television tour of the palace. Caroline, unlike the Kennedy daughter who was kept out of sight on the White House tour, was shown in the family's private zoo. Also in the show a parrot sang Monaco's national anthem. In later years Caroline would dine and go to discos in New York with Bobby Shriver, Jr., a Kennedy relative and pal. The Kelly side of the family resembled the Kennedys. Both the Kellys and the Kennedys were Irish-American, self-made, and highly competitive. The kind of jock attitude that characterized both families pitted one sibling against the other for the parents' approval. Only in America could a dynasty, à la the Kennedys, be so short on heritage and history.

Both princesses attended the local Catholic school, Pensionnat Les Dammas de Saint Maur, where they were taught in French. One of Stephanie's teachers observed: "First she was a naughty girl, then she was a good girl. She probably exaggerated both her goodness and her naughtiness. She was an interesting child, an original little girl, striking rather than pretty, her face had a chiseled look, definitely from the Kelly side."

Whereas Stephanie's willfulness was more like a

childish outburst, Caroline's behavior seemed more directed. "Caroline always had a strong willful personality and would not hesitate to speak her mind," Nanny King explains. "She takes after the prince more than her mother."

Stephanie maintains that there was discipline even at Christmastime. "We had to deserve what we got," she explains. "It was never a question of just saying, 'I want this.' I remember finding a chunk of coal in my Christmas stocking one year because I had not been a good girl." The children also had to observe strict table manners. "When anyone in our family had elbows on the table," Caroline reports, "Our grandmother jabbed them with a fork." As little girls their bedtime was 6:30 P.M.

The two princesses were encouraged to help people less fortunate. Grace and her girls, according to Father Jacobs, went in their blue jeans and workclothes to paint the walls and clean the floors in the homes of Monaco's poor and shut-in old ladies. As a young adult Caroline would go on to start a hot line to help local teenagers who might be suicidal, pregnant, or on drugs. She also assisted a French priest in Brittany who had a sailboat where children on drugs got help.

At fourteen, Caroline was sent off to St. Mary's, Ascot, England, a Catholic boarding school. With its emphasis on teaching charm and manners to girls from arch English-Catholic families, St. Mary's could not have been more different from the Mediterranean spirit. Years later Caroline would remember how the nuns made the girls cross the street "like little soldiers" if boys approached their side of the street. On school breaks Caroline sometimes stayed with Phyllis Earl, an American woman who had once been Grace's private secretary. "Various boys would come by the house," Earl remembers. "It always amazed me how quickly she saw through phonies. She was always self-sufficient and very, very coolly precocious."

By the time she was eighteen Caroline more than made up for the stifling discipline at St. Mary's. There would be no more starchy uniforms in her wardrobe. She had her eighteenth-birthday dress, a Karl Lagerfeld creation, altered to expose her cleavage. Caroline also got a blue Fiat for that birthday. Though officially enrolled in the Institut d'Etudes Politiques, it seemed, according to press accounts, like she attended Disco Tech more often, with several royally unsuitable men. The princess denied such reports. "I only get out to a party once a month —maybe not that often—but the press will sometimes use my head on someone else's body for a picture. I've sued for that."

To supervise her daughter more closely, Grace spent much of her time at the family's Paris apartment on Avenue Foch, a large, sunny place with thick French windows that blotted out the traffic noises. Next door to them lived internationally celebrated classical pianist Arthur Rubinstein and his wife, Polish-born Nela, a warm, spirited woman, and author of a cookbook, whom the girls liked a great deal. Nela's Bavarian cream recipe was a favorite of Grace's and her girls. Grace traveled with Nela to Salzburg, Austria, for the music festivals there. Around the Grimaldi home, though, rock music, courtesy of ten-year-old Stephanie, dominated, and Grace had to ask her frequently to turn down the decibel level. Caroline, called "Grimmy" by classmates and also nicknamed "Max the Menace," after a short-tempered French cartoon character, was reportedly studying much of the time. "Three hours every night and ten to thirteen hours over the week-end," Caroline told a UPI interviewer back in 1975. "My own ambition is to keep on being a student for a while. There is so much to learn—isn't there? And then someday to be able to use my languages, French, English, German, and Spanish. Maybe at international conferences as an interpreter. I love to travel." Her first-year courses: economics, finance, international relations, and constitutional law. "They say about twenty percent are going to quit before the term ends," she reported then. "And only fifty percent of the rest will pass."

Caroline, notwithstanding her apparent intelligence and linguistic abilities, ended up in never-never land, the wrong fifty percent. She did not pass her exam.

By then Caroline knew a thing or two about shopping. When it came to fashion she took her mother's directive well. Caroline, with Stephanie quick to follow, graced the Houses of Dior and Chloé, both as client and pal. Whereas they were clothed as children in the elegantly simple and pure designs of celebrated American designer the late Florence Eiseman, from Milwaukee, as young adults they graduated to the haute couture creations. Dior's Marc Bohan would squire Grace and later Caroline to society balls. He would eventually hire Stephanie to apprentice as an assistant designer. The girls also liked Valentino and Ungaro. For jewelry and evening bags, Caroline buzzed into Bulgari's. On top of many of these expenses, which were covered by the prince, who has a reported personal wealth of about $500 million, they also had allowances. Their coiffure was attended to by the crown prince of stylists, Alexandre of Paris, originator of the beehive and artichoke hairdos. Grace was a long-time client there. Even at a young age, the princesses were cloaked in the finest. At twelve, according to a *New York Times* fashion story on furs for children, Caroline had a rabbit coat; and Stephanie, at four, had been seen in ermine. The princesses developed an enduring passion for shopping. From fourteen on, Caroline saved all her shoes, and says she has a passion for them. She wears a different pair every day. Their favorite makeup: a suntan.

They did exhibit some individualism, though, by donning jeans, T-shirts, and Spandex tops. This was a form of rebellion in that their father had put his foot down when it came to Grace wearing pants. She was only allowed to do so at the beach or in the garden. "My husband disapproves of pants," Grace once revealed. "He doesn't appreciate it when women come for lunch in trousers." It would be Princess Caroline who, at eighteen, proclaimed Karl Lagerfeld "leader of left-wing designers—he is my favorite." Of course, she was speaking from the front lines of fashion— certainly not political battle.

Her next academic experience would take place at the Sorbonne where, after dropping out for a year to attend to her marriage and Monaco's UNICEF Year of the Child events, she would ultimately complete a degree in philosophy and child psychology. One area in which she needed no schooling, it would turn out, was in being a Mediterranean princess. Charming and comfortable with herself, she absorbed the style of European royalty, inherited from her father's side, without the conflicts of an Irish-American family like the Kellys, striving to improve their financial and social position through hard work.

Taking a cue from her older sister, Stephanie also did not fare well at school. At sixteen, she was packed off to St. Dominique's girls school in Paris, where her mother hoped the strict lights-out-at-ten-o'clock regimen would provide some necessary discipline.

This was not to be. Two days into her first term there, Stephanie was caught smoking and riding a motor scooter around Paris. She was promptly expelled. "Her behavior," a school official primly announced, "is incompatible with the rules."

As the youngest, Stephanie would end up a beneficiary of her parents' experiences with Caroline. Instead of enrolling her in St. Mary's, the rigid English school that may have contributed to Caroline's later rebelliousness, the Grimaldis sent her to the co-ed lycée Charles de Foucauld. "I was happier there," Stephanie says. Indeed, the results suggested this. Stephanie passed her *baccalauréat* before her eighteenth birthday. A proud and delighted Grace at the time wrote to a friend these words: "I am out of school."

In no time so was Stephanie. "The idea of university bores me," she declared. Much like Caroline before her—who gave up an opportunity to attend Princeton—Stephanie opted for the school of life that lay beyond the palace gates.

As Caroline reflected later in an essay she penned for the British *Tatler* in 1981: "Monaco is a small town and everybody knows everybody else. By the time we reached our teen years, we longed for some kind of action. It was not only boring. We were too protected. When would we be allowed to escape? Where was the adventure we deserved?"

CHAPTER 3

The Princess and the Playboy

Nobody promised more adventure than Philippe Junot. Much like any young woman wanting to get out from under her parents' control, Caroline saw Junot as her ticket to freedom. Parisian boulevardier, sometime businessman, and sports enthusiast, Junot was seventeen years older than the princess. The Grimaldis were worried parents, with higher ambitions for their daughter in the marriage department. Though hardly in the same royal stratosphere as the Windsors, the Grimaldis wanted a suitably aristocratic suitor to uphold their dynastic tradition.

Junot was not the man they had in mind for their firstborn daughter. Grace described his occupation thus: "He works with banks." They worried that he might be a fortune hunter. Junot called himself a "financial adviser," though details of his work life, said to include a stint with Jack in the Box fast foods, remained sketchy. His biggest triumphs, it seemed, had to do with fast cars, race horses, and above all, women. Certainly, "playboy" was not an acceptable title for the husband of a princess.

But in the summer of 1976 at Régine's in Paris, she thought her prince had come. Instead of sweeping her off her feet, though, Junot took a verbal swipe at her. Squeezing one of her arms, bared by an off-the-shoulder evening gown, he told her that she could stand to lose a few pounds. "Come on, fatty," Junot was heard to say as they were leaving.

It seemed the perfect way to serenade Her Serene Highness, by now bored with all the fawning and flattery from others. "He was the first one not to look at her like a princess," recalls cousin Christian de Massy. "He treated her as if she were anybody. Caroline has such a big ego that she thought, 'I've got to get this guy.' " His carefree ways seemed an antidote to the conventlike atmosphere at St. Mary's in Ascot.

Though Junot implied that he might have some blue blood in his background, there was no evidence to back up this claim. His father, a wealthy deputy mayor of Paris, had been chairman of the French division of Westinghouse. His parents were divorced. They were a perfectly respectable, if not distinguished, upper-middle-class family. Trouble was, their son Philippe did not share the same work ethic.

"The dregs are always around," sniffs Vera Maxwell, "when there is money and a name involved. Junot was awful. Even Caroline's wayward sister, Stephanie, took an instant dislike to Junot. About the only family relative or friend who seemed to welcome Caroline's beau was cousin Christian de Massy, who had met him a year before. "I like Junot," he says. "He's fun. He didn't invent electricity or a new chemical formula. But he was a good guy. He was in Monaco to have a party, and a party he had!" However, de Massy's motivation may have been partly selfish. By his own admission, the so-called black sheep of the Grimaldis found that Rainier's fury now became focused more on Junot than himself.

An ideal son-in-law, according to Grace, was somebody like Prince Henri of Luxembourg. Whether or not the prince himself was interested, Caroline proclaimed him "a bore." Prince Charles of England, another frequently mentioned prospect, was clearly beyond the social grasp of the Grimaldis. For one thing, as a member of the Church of England, Charles would not have married a Catholic. Further, the proper English tradition might not merge well with the Grimaldis' Mediterranean heritage. In any event, Caroline was not to run into Charles in the jet-set circles she traveled. As it would turn out, Charles did not attend Caroline's wedding. The official line was that he had other engagements. The British press, however, interpreted his absence as a royal snub.

In a way it made more sense that Caroline would meet a playboy than a prince. After all, she grew up in one of the world's priciest playgrounds. Despite the cultural activities promoted by Grace, which took place largely in the summer months, Monte Carlo was a resort town, with hotels and condos littering the landscape. No one encouraged development more than the prince himself. Children of some of the world's wealthiest men satisfied their every hedonistic whim here. As in most resort communities, distinctions between bona-fide heirs and pretenders to great fortunes or family backgrounds tended to blur under a blazing sun. But always, the great equalizer would be the disco, which, despite its pseudoelitist admission policies, often attracted the kings and queens of Eurotrash.

Quite the sportive type, Junot was brought up, like Caroline, on the Côte d'Azur. An all-around athlete, he captained an amateur football team whose members included Jean-Paul Belmondo. Before a serious accident he had been a rally driver. He was also an accomplished skier and tennis player. His academic credentials were less clear-cut, though he did, like Caroline, attend the Institute of Political Science for a time. He put in some time, he claimed, learning about business on the New York Stock Exchange and other world financial centers including Brussels and London. At the time of his engagement to Caroline, Junot described himself as a "financial adviser" to clients in New York and Montreal. Whatever, he had a certain currency with women who found him witty, fun-loving, and attractive. Junot was viewed more as a card-carrying member of a vanishing breed of European playboy than a man with a brilliant future. "Philippe is a good guy to have a drink with," says a friend. "Nobody could stand up and say they saw him in an office though."

Grace saw mostly heartache ahead for her daughter. She could not have failed to notice that Caroline —just like the young Grace Kelly—looked to an older man for help in her quest for independence. At the same time she wanted to spare Caroline the agony that she had suffered at the hands of her own parents, particularly her father, whose interference wrecked several of her romances. Her desire to marry Oleg Cassini who, incidentally, had given Grace a romantic whirl around the Riviera long before she met and married Rainier, had been dashed by her parents. She later bowed out of her own accord. Though a celebrated international fashion designer and twice-divorced by then, Cassini did share one trait in common with the chronically unproductive bachelor Junot—they were both free spirits capable of enormous *joie de vivre.*

Such an adventurous spirit was in sharp contrast to Rainier's stuffy, anachronistic ways. As Grace once told an interviewer: "Here the man is definitely the master of the house, and there are no two ways about it. My husband is still shocked by the way some of my American friends behave in front of their husbands, contradicting them. We would never do that here."

Hardly the life of the party, the prince was frequently caught snoozing at the symphony or ballet. His idea of a holiday might be checking into a posh health farm to shed the extra pounds he picked up at charity dinners. "Rainier sleeps a lot, looks at TV, and plays golf," his nephew de Massy reports. "He can be very amusing—he loves dirty jokes—but he takes himself very seriously. Monaco is smaller than New York's Central Park. Mayor Koch at least takes a laugh at himself." A trip to New York, when Caroline and Albert were still small, may further illustrate Rainier's enthusiasms. While the children nursed colds in the family's suite at the Regency Hotel, Grace visited art galleries while Rainier attended the circus here. His curiosity did not match his seemingly limitless funds. Except for a cruise in the Galapagos Islands, one of the more exotic trips was white-water rafting on the Snake River. There were no African safaris, crocodile hunts in South America, or visits to China on the family's itinerary. The summer of Caroline's nineteenth year, when the family took a swing through America's West, Rainier had announced previously, "We promised the children that they would not have to vacation in Philadelphia this year." In New Mexico, another stop on their tour, they stayed at a luxury health resort outside Santa Fe near a Pueblo Indian settlement, because that way, to Rainier's thinking, they could be close to the Indian culture. Against this background, Caroline would honeymoon with Junot on the South Sea islands.

In a sense Caroline's honeymoon—from palace and convent strictures—began before she met Junot. A week after turning eighteen she was spotted at a Parisian club, L'Aventure, in a white Lagerfeld gown, a birthday gift from her parents, that she apparently had had altered and now wore practically down to her navel. On account of her heavy makeup *Paris Match* added another title to the ones that she already had. "A Vamp of Eighteen Years," they spoofed. The man she was with that night caught hell, as it were, from the Grimaldis. That man, Philippe Lanville, a songwriter in his mid-twenties, would also take the flak when Caroline later flunked her finals at the Institute of Political Science. He eventually bowed out of his association with the princess. "Our friendship is over," he told the press. "We've had no quarrel . . . I am sick of having no identity of my own. I cannot go on being an appendage of Caroline. I have no time for singing or anything else. So now I am calling it finished. I will return to leading a normal life like ordinary people. It will be marvelous to be divorced from all the fuss which attends every move Caroline makes." Their five-month relationship was said then to be the longest in her repertoire. Other suitors were reported to include a British playboy in his thirties, who sent pink roses to Grace that were promptly returned.

Another admirer, Julien Clerc, a French West Indian, had appeared nude in the rock-opera *Hair*. Owing to his popularity in France, Clerc played the Sporting Club in Monte Carlo. During Clerc's run there, the prince took Caroline on a ten-day cruise to the Balearics. That relationship was now fini.

Philippe, however, was hardly one to do a disappearing act in the face of disapproval. Quite the contrary, he seemed to turn up everywhere. Junot, with no pressing work at the moment, had plenty of time to court Caroline. He seemed, in fact, to make a career out of this. In early 1977 he asked her to marry him. Caroline accepted. In March the prince allowed Caroline to travel alone to Ibiza with Philippe. At Easter the family received him at Roc Agel. He returned to Monaco for a tennis tournament and the Grand Prix. By July, Philippe joined the family on a cruise to the Galapagos Islands. Rainier's consent was hardly forthcoming. He acted swiftly to try to dissuade her. Not wanting to close out communication with their daughter by refusing her permission, they asked her, just as Grace's parents had done with the Cassini affair, to give herself more time. After all, they reminded Caroline, she was still young and had plans to get a university degree. Surprisingly, the princess and her beau agreed.

Not one to capitulate to anyone's demands, royal or otherwise, Junot seemed to flaunt Rainier's authority. Photographs of them aboard a yacht with Junot kissing Caroline's bare breasts appeared around the world. Whereas in the past Grimaldi functionaries managed to buy negatives of pictures—the next best thing to arresting journalists (which they had managed once with an Italian editor)—this time the photos, taken with a hidden camera, were irretrievable. Caroline and Junot, summoned to Rainier's study, got a royal dressing-down from him. Though duly respectful and apologetic for the moment, they carried on their romance nonetheless. Some observers theorize that with the publication of these photos, Junot was able to force Rainier's hand in granting an engagement. Whether or not that was the case, the couple got permission to be engaged, but only on the condition they wait a year to marry.

Before Junot's arrival on the scene, it was thought that Caroline would benefit from a university education in the United States. There, the princess would get a taste of campus life, far more innocent and insulating than the life she was leading at Paris night spots. The place they had picked out for her was Princeton University in New Jersey, within commuting distance of Grace's native Philadelphia. But after meeting Philippe, the princess scotched that plan. Instead she would study toward a bachelor's degree in psychology at the Sorbonne in Paris. There she would divide her time between her parents' home on the Avenue Foch and Philippe's apartment.

Caroline held steadfastly, however, to her marriage plan. Nine months after the engagement they asked her parents' consent again. Apparently, the Grimaldis' stalling technique had worn thin. With Caroline fast approaching her twenty-first birthday, they could no longer argue against her age. Originally, she had promised that she would not get hitched before then and had kept to this. Grace then asked Rainier to forbid the marriage. The prince's threatened ban backfired. Caroline agreed to it. No problem, the princess replied coolly, she would live with Philippe out of wedlock. Her response spelled more problems for the prince. "Living in sin," which would now be the case, would not play well in Catholic Monaco. With great worry and sorrow, as well as anger, they agreed to the marriage. "Rainier hated him, mistrusted him, considered him a fortune hunter," de Massy says.

Usually Grace laid down the law, as it were, with her. Because Rainier doted on his daughters, Grace was often forced to balance his indulgences with some form of discipline. "I think Grace was an incredible woman," says her friend Vera Maxwell. "She was extremely good at making her husband feel important. She deferred to Rainier—women do this with husbands—and yet she did it all. He had a terrible temper. She was strict with the children, but always in a decisive and meaningful way."

As a result there was often friction between mother and daughter. As Caroline once told the British magazine *Woman*, "I can't stand carrying the burden of her unrealized ambitions." She also revealed in this rare unguarded moment that she would tease Grace about her silver-screen kisses, to which her mother responded by "rushing to her room in a temper." "I wonder," Caroline added caustically, "if it was to leaf through the scrapbook she keeps up there." To another magazine Caroline described her mother thus: "She has a Nordic temperament. She is very beautiful, but this kind of beauty can be sometimes rather cold."

Caroline hero-worshipped her father and felt more sympathetic to his Mediterranean temperament. If the prince could not crack her resolve, then nobody else would succeed. The only logical move then was to sanction the wedding.

It would not be the first Grimaldi union to create unpleasant feelings. Rainier's wedding to Grace, daughter of a bricklayer from Philadelphia, had been boycotted by European royalty. But unlike Caroline, her father broke off a previously intended marriage to French actress Gisèle Pascal after a six-year liaison. The reason was that she would not be able to give him an heir. The fertility report had been wrong—Pascal later married and had a child. Then there was Caroline's grandmother Princess Charlotte, known as the "Madcap Princess of Monaco," who ran off with an Italian physician. And there was a Monaco folk legend as well about a thirteenth-century witch who condemned all Grimaldis to unhappy marriages. A more immediate omen had to do with the forty-two-foot $250,000 catamaran that the prince was having delivered as a wedding gift. On its voyage from Southampton, England, to Monaco via the inland waterways, it reportedly ran aground. No one told the skipper that part of France's Canal du Midi was being drained.

A church wedding between the twenty-one-year-old princess and the thirty-eight-year-old playboy took place on June 29, 1978. No mishaps occurred at the wedding, perhaps the least strained moment for the Grimaldis in the two-year courtship of their daughter. Though her heart was heavy with doubt and worry, Grace did not allow her mood to dampen the day. It would prove to be one of her best performances. Grace put on an affair to remember, with some of the same splendor that had attended her own wedding.

After the exchange of rings Junot bowed in front of Rainier, who stared icily at the air. Throughout the marriage Junot would be required to call his father-in-law "Your Highness." Grace, blinking back tears, managed a smile. The only hitch in the ceremony: the couple had trouble fitting the wedding rings on each others' fingers. The princess began to giggle. "Hey," Junot whispered, "relax your finger." Monsignor Gilles Barthe, who had baptized Caroline and married her parents while bishop of the principality, performed the church wedding. Caroline wore a white embroidered Dior dress with a hairpiece of silk flowers. Grace also wore a Dior creation, a yellow dress, with a matching wide-brimmed hat.

The rehearsal was no ordinary drill. It was filmed by the prince as cameraman, and Grace as the director. Actor David Niven would turn up to offer his opinion. Niven also hosted a prenuptial lunch at his Cap Ferrat villa. But the highlight of the prenuptial festivities was the palace ball the night before the wedding. Caroline, wearing a tiara borrowed from her mother and a beatific smile, danced to a rendition of "Sweet Caroline," performed by a pop group. Stephanie boycotted the ball. With no special fondness for Junot, she vowed at the time that she would never marry a Frenchman. Of course, there had to be a reason for her no-show and the reason was that her mother refused to allow her to attend the ball in jeans. After all, this was a princess always up for fun, even if it meant sometimes opening Tiffany's, a Monte Carlo "dive" where she sometimes served as hatcheck girl and waitress as well.

If Caroline's choice of marriage partner did little to advance the prestige of the royal family, at least the guest list at the ball suggested how far Rainier had arrived since his marriage over twenty years before to Grace. It was a marriage of European and Hollywood royalty. Frank Sinatra, Ava Gardner, Cary Grant, and Gregory Peck were among Grace's Hollywood loyalists. The principality now attracted an array of titled Europeans: former King Umberto of Italy, the Count and Countess of Barcelona, the Count and Countess of Paris, the ex-King of Romania, Prince Bertil and Princess Lilian of Sweden, and former King Constantine of Greece and his wife, Anne-Marie.

Absent this time, though, were the press, except for Grace's personal friend, photographer Howell Conant, who had snapped the exclusive shots of Caroline as a newborn. Grace remembered well how the press had made her wedding day a misery. Two weeks after her wedding, Caroline held a press conference while on honeymoon in Mooréa to answer reports that her wedding was too small. "I was not getting married for the public," she snorted. "I didn't want my own wedding to be a three-ring circus. It's my own personal affair. I don't care what the world says. It was a beautiful wedding because I had the people I love and wanted to be there. The press is upset, but that's tough."

At the reception following the wedding Caroline and Philippe grinned broadly as the band played "Happy Days Are Here Again" on the palace parade ground. There was a six-tiered wedding cake with two captive doves trapped in their makeshift cage between the fifth and sixth layers. Some forty-three Monégasques, born the same year as Caroline, were among the three hundred guests at the reception. Wedding presents ranged from a South American bird trained to whistle a few bars of Monaco's national anthem to pots, pans, luggage and silver boxes, a silk rug from the Aga Khan, plus the yacht and a new apartment from the bride's parents. Junot's father gave them a Louis XIV desk which he said that he had received from his own father.

After the civil ceremony the day before in the throne room, some four thousand locals attended a reception given by Rainier in the palace courtyard. The newlyweds appeared on the balcony as guests below had high tea followed by champagne and pizza. Though the principality comprises fewer than five hundred acres, some Monégasques claimed that this was the first time they came face-to-face with Princess Caroline.

They would get another glimpse of her after the church ceremony. Caroline and Philippe walked through the ancient cobblestoned streets to the Chapel of the Misericorde. There, according to custom, Caroline left her bouquet of stephanotis as a gesture of piety before the statue of the Virgin. Then it was off to the Town Hall, where locals presented them with a two-hundred-piece silver set. They rode back to the palace in a limousine.

What was supposed to be a three-week honeymoon in Tahiti stretched into an extended holiday in Greece, Scotland, the West Indies, and the United States over the next two years. Caroline and Philippe were installed in a penthouse apartment in the Avenue Bosquet, close to the Eiffel Tower and with the Champs-de-Mars, a favorite gathering place for mothers with prams, below their window. Though Caroline announced previously at her Moorea island honeymoon press conference that she hoped to have four children, no little Philippes seemed to be on the horizon. Perhaps Caroline—despite herself—heeded her mother's advice. "I was twenty-eight when Caroline was born," Grace said at the time of the wedding. "I adore children, but I hope Caroline will not experience motherhood immediately."

For a time the couple calmed down, staying at home to dine on her hamburgers, braised rabbit, and cheesecake. Ironically, this was the same girl who had objected to taking a six-week course at Maxim's cooking school in preparing tables, selecting silverware, and generally playing hostess. In a *Time* magazine profile of Caroline, she was reported to have responded to her mother's Maxim's suggestion thus: "Mother, we've got slaves for that." Yet Caroline was not entirely comfortable with her new role as a wife.

At first when there was a phone call for "Madame Junot" the princess would hang up, believing it was the wrong number. "I'm still surprised when someone calls me Madame," she admitted then. "I think they're talking to someone else."

Of Caroline's marriage a friend remarked, "Now that she's become a woman, Caroline can be a kid again. She's out of her mother's shadows." Hardly a hausfrau, Caroline continued to frequent her and Philippe's favorite nightspots. Around the principality, too, Philippe was the life of the party. Rainier, however, never found his son-in-law amusing. He more or less froze him out. By nature reserved and unable to communicate easily, Rainier, if he was displeased with Junot, as was often the case, would communicate this through a palace aide. On one occasion, a relative recalls, Rainier's secretary arrived on a motorbike to tell Junot that the prince was annoyed, only moments after his son-in-law had left the palace. Further, Junot would be returning there a half hour later as well as the next day for a party.

But the princess always kept one foot in the palace. She took a year off from the Sorbonne to chair Monaco's UNICEF Year of the Child Committee. In October 1978, she and Philippe, both in T-shirts, led a walkathon through Monaco to raise money for children. The next year, in February 1979, Caroline appeared on a chat show dealing with the problems of youth. After all, Monaco's teens were not immune to drugs, depression, suicide, and divorce.

Soon the princess would be faced with her own problem, namely Junot's infidelities, which, according to some close associates, had begun even as their honeymoon ended. Reports of his indiscretions across the Atlantic reached her. One photographer snapped Junot dancing at New York's Studio 54 with an ex-girlfriend when he had told Caroline he was in Montreal on business. By spring of 1980, the princess could no longer turn her head to his dalliances in Paris, New York, and even Monte Carlo. She was so upset that she confessed to her mother that her marriage was in trouble. Grace offered her practical advice without any "I-told-you-so's." She also summoned Caroline's cousin, Grace Le Vine, to come from Philadelphia to Monaco to console the heartbroken princess. "She really did love him," Le Vine told author James Spada. "She was a wreck when it broke up. She was devastated." Caroline began spending more time at the palace. By June the couple had separated. But the world would not know until August at the annual Red Cross Ball, the most important social event of the season, attended by some one thousand celebrity guests and socialites. Junot, meanwhile, was fourteen hundred miles away in Turkey with the beautiful young daughter of a Costa Rican diplomat. After Grace and Albert opened the ball, Caroline, glum and subdued, remained at her table instead of joining her father on the dance floor next.

An announcement followed the next day. "Caroline will get over it," palace spokesperson Nadia Lacoste predicted. "She is not one to let her arms dangle. It is a united family, and they will protect her as they have always done in the past." Her typically sugar-coated remarks did little to alleviate Caroline's pain and humiliation, exacerbated by an announcement earlier that same day from her soon-to-be ex-husband halfway around the world. "Everything is finished between Caroline and me," Junot said. "We are both free to do as we please." He also identified his companion, the diplomat's daughter, as his secretary.

Soon after Grace paid a visit to the Vatican to try to get an annulment. To this day the Pope has yet to grant one. The problem, in part, was the couple's high profile. A papal declaration of nullity has always been influenced by discretion on the part of a couple. Caroline, now the dutiful daughter, gave up her visits to Régine's Monte Carlo disco, Jimmy Z's, and beach clubs where she suns herself, as a form of atonement. Junot, meanwhile, carried on as usual. Rainier's ban on any communication between Caroline and Philippe, according to London gossip columnist Nigel Dempster, was violated by both of them. Nonetheless, on October 9, 1980, six days after filing, a divorce was granted.

Whether or not Junot made out like one of the one-arm bandits in the Monte Carlo casino remains a mystery. Whatever the settlement, it was apparently sufficient to keep Philippe from playing kiss-and-tell. Asked some time after the divorce by de Massy how much he was paid to keep quiet, Junot said, "Shut up —leave me my eye." There were rumors that Junot turned down a million-dollar book advance, as well as a hundred-thousand-dollar fee from a tabloid newspaper, to present his side of the story. Recently remarried, Junot continues to turn up in Europe's resort areas, including Marbella, where he seemed to be on an extended vacation last year.

But Princess Caroline would have the last word. Calling the marriage her chief regret in life, she told Barbara Walters in a September 1985 interview: "I wouldn't have married so young the first time. But I wanted to get away from home, so it seemed a rather classical way of doing it." She added: "I wasn't allowed to go live on my own. I had to live at home with my parents, so I had to find the next best way of convincing them."

Ironically, Caroline's lust for adventure led her right back to the palace that she had tried to escape from in the first place.

CHAPTER 4

Grace's Death

THE whole of the Grimaldi family loved to spend much of the summer months at Roc Agel. It represented for them the happiest of times. They could be alone or with only their closest friends at this home. Most importantly, the paparazzi were nowhere around, out of sight and out of mind, finally.

But as events would transpire in the summer of 1982, the world would show up on their doorstep. An accident took place that would change the face of the Grimaldi family forever. On September 13, Princess Grace had a car crash that ultimately claimed her life. Instantly the press swooped down on them again. First reports minimized the extent of Grace's injuries. Later, stories of a cover-up would emerge.

Some reports suggested that instead of using a driver, Grace drove alone with Stephanie. That way there would be room for Stephanie's dresses to lie flat on the backseat of the car, a British Rover 3500. Some accounts said that Grace took the wheel of the car even though she had given up driving after a previous accident some years before. "She was a terrible driver," said Rupert Allen, a close friend of the royal family's. "Her mind was always someplace else." Grace was a slow, careful driver, and if she offered to take the children down in the car, they would usually react by telling her, "No, we'll go by foot. We'll get there quicker."

A rumor that placed Stephanie in the driver's seat spread fast. Even Grace's long-standing friend Vera Maxwell maintains to this day: "Stephanie—as everybody knows—was the cause of her mother's death. Stephanie was a novice driver. She has a temper and her father spoiled her. Her mother let her drive an old gear-shift car, and they came across from this tiny country road to a main highway. They went over the road and down a ravine and they hit a tree." The week before the accident Maxwell was visiting with the family at Roc Agel. "Stephanie was learning to drive," she reports. "She was in the car all the time. Her mother wanted her to learn." At the time of Grace's death, Maxwell had already returned to the States. She turned around and went immediately back to Monaco for the funeral. Maxwell, however, quickly adds: "I think the father [Rainier] was quite right to put it out that the mother [Grace] had had an embolism, and that it was not Stephanie's fault as many people were saying. It was a terrible tragedy. I think all the children feel the loss of their mother deeply. But I think Stephanie needed her mother more than anyone would suspect. At this age you need your mother more. The father was very attached to and spoiled Stephanie, but the mother was there all the time."

The living room of Maxwell's New York apartment is today practically a shrine to Princess Grace. On the coffee table there is a miniature photo album of Grace and her children with a picture of Grace in the snow. Hanging on the walls are more shots, including an autographed picture of Caroline. Maxwell also has the number 10 original print of one of Grace's pressed flower arrangements. Their friendship went back a long time. Maxwell provided some of Grace's clothes when she was an actress on Broadway. Later they would meet in Dallas, Texas, at the "Oscars" of fashion, a Neiman-Marcus awards ceremony. The year was 1955, when Maxwell was one of the honorees. It was just after Grace had met Rainier. "We didn't want to stay for the reception after," Maxwell recalls. "All these cowboys kept coming up. She asked me to go upstairs with her because she was waiting for a call from Rainier. We had adjoining suites. She was very much in love with Rainier." Maxwell would later attend Caroline's christening, and visit frequently after that.

Christian de Massy argues adamantly against the theory that Stephanie was driving. "Not for one minute would Grace have let her drive," he insists. "Grace was such a God-fearing, respectful woman. And no way would she do anything illegal in France. She wouldn't drive into Monaco and have the police saluting when the kid hasn't got a license." He adds: "Rainier screwed up. He came and had the car covered up and pulled back to Monaco. Then people started thinking, 'Hey, this was fast.'"

Early news reports proved to be both sketchy and contradictory due, in part, to the absence of chief press officer Nadia Lacoste, reported to be in Germany then. *The New York Times* headlined a September 13 UPI story: "Princess Grace Breaks Thigh." Half the palace employees as well were on holiday.

The official account of the accident had Grace suffering a stroke and losing control of the car during the twelve-mile trip through the coastal mountains.

The Rover went off the inner end of the crash barrier and somersaulted down a forty-meter drop, and landed with its wheels in the air on a small plateau of market gardens. Moments later, Stephanie was heard wailing, "Maman is dead . . . you must help Maman." Then to the owner of a house by the market gardens, she pleaded, "You must warn Papa!" To which the owner responded, "Who is your papa?" Stephanie said, "He's the prince. I'm his daughter. Maman is in the car." With only the first reports to go on, Monaco and the rest of the world were led to believe that their beloved Princess Grace would soon recover. Inside the Princess Grace Hospital, however, those involved began to realize that the accident was far more serious.

According to Sarah Bradford, a biographer of the late princess, after the head surgeon there examined Grace in the emergency room, he reported that she reacted to pain, but not when anyone spoke to her. Further, her lung had collapsed, and there was both blood and air in the thorax, the latter presumably caused by her falling against the steering wheel, adding credence to the theory that Grace had been driving at the time of the accident.

Barely conscious upon arrival, Grace was hooked up immediately to a life-support system. Her brain was constantly monitored. At some point the scan indicated that Grace had suffered a slight stroke, exacerbated by a wound to her forehead and other injuries such as the blood and air in the thorax already mentioned. That night Grace went into an even deeper coma. By the following afternoon, the monitor showed that all brain activity had ceased. Princess Grace was technically dead. Later that evening, at 10:30 P.M., nearly thirty-six hours after Grace had been brought in there, Prince Rainier with his only son, Albert, and eldest daughter, Caroline, at his side gave the doctors permission to turn off the life-support system.

Stephanie, meanwhile, lay in a state of shock in another part of the hospital. Unaware of her mother's death, she told her doctor about how she had tried to stop the car from crashing by pulling on the hand-brake. Caroline, who had rushed back from the Deauville Film Festival the moment she got news of the accident, now took charge. Initially, it did not seem as though it would be fatal. In fact, Prince Rainier himself had told his sister Princess Antoinette, who rang up from Scotland upon hearing about the crash, that there was no need to hurry back. While trying to console her father, Caroline also managed the funeral arrangements for her mother. By then palace staff members had cut short their holidays to help the grieving family.

As writer Peter Gallico's wife, Virginia, told Bradford, "The gardeners were up all night collecting and arranging flowers." There were flowers everywhere. The large courtyard, which could accommodate some fifty cars, was completely strewn with them. "Not huge bouquets," one observer said, "but tiny little flowers handpicked by Monégasques."

Father Peter Jacobs, a close friend of Grace's, arrived in Monaco from New York on Thursday and went immediately to pay his respects. He would conduct a private mass on Friday evening for the family. Also present were Nela Rubinstein, Grace's Paris neighbor and close friend; Secretary of the Navy John F. Lehman, Jr., a cousin of Grace's; and other Kelly relatives. Paul Belmondo, son of the French actor Jean-Paul Belmondo, who had rushed from Paris to be at Stephanie's bedside, was also there.

It was at this moment that Father Jacobs noticed

how spiritual Caroline was. "I've been a priest for thirty years," he says, "and sometimes when you meet somebody like Mother Teresa, you know that something is different. I noticed that in Caroline. I really believe there is really something deeply spiritual about her. I sensed that when talking to her. And the way she said her rosaries made a lasting impression. I wish I could express what I saw . . . the way she acted in the chapel when no else was there . . . like a nun, deeply spiritual, not faking it."

Indeed, no one had to manufacture any grief. Grace's death touched not only those who were close to her, but also her many admirers around the world. In the midst of this outpouring of affection and loss, there was another press stampede on the principality. Nadia Lacoste, resuming her duties upon her return from Germany, struggled to combat rumors of a cover-up.

Why, for example, hadn't the full seriousness of Grace's accident been made public from the start? Rumors about Stephanie driving the car now included a theory that because she was legally underage, palace officials were covering it up. One of the more outrageous theories held that the Nice Mafia, angry about being kept out of Monte Carlo, had tampered with the car. Blame was also aimed at the hospital for what was called inadequate medical facilities.

Skepticism remains to this day. Countering the Stephanie stories, one witness, staying at Roc Agel at the time, insisted that Grace was at the wheel as he followed her in his own car. In a *Life* interview several months after Grace's death, Prince Rainier admitted to being disturbed by press skepticism and said he could not understand why people would not accept the official explanation.

"All right," he told the magazine, "there are circumstances where you can't understand how somebody could go off the road in a place that seemed very far from any kind of surprises. There is a question mark there, so the only explanation is that there was some form of eclipse, that she lost control of the car. Stephanie has told me only one thing about the accident. I didn't want to press her. Of course, maybe some day she'll be more talkative. One can feel that she's closed off on the subject. But she did say to me, 'Oh, Mommy panicked. Mommy panicked.' . . . Stephanie was serious when she said, 'Oh, Mommy panicked. She didn't know what to do. She lost control.' "

Back in November 1982, two months after Grace's death, palace spokesperson Lacoste stated tersely: "Stephanie is still alive, and she has her life in front of her." Later on, the princess herself would get to the point: "I'm fed up with people saying I killed my mother," she told at least one reporter.

Monégasques would never forget the day that Princess Grace was laid to rest. Saturday, the eighteenth of September 1982, was one of the saddest days in the history of the principality. Swollen with sorrow, Prince Rainier, with Caroline and Albert at his side, led the funeral cortege through the pink and ocher streets of Monaco to the cathedral where twenty-six years before he had married Grace Kelly and later their children had been baptized.

The New York Times report was at once lyrical and surreal. John Vinocur wrote: "In the Mediterranean sun, there were few of the usual somber props of mourning. Instead, the soft blue sky, the pastel walls of the prince's palace, the red-plumed helmets of Monaco's carabiniers, the backdrop of palms and cactus and bright water, gave the black-suited figures of the funeral a vivid, almost wild sadness." The article went on to observe further: "The sorrow was affecting, intense, real. In a tiny place, once best known for a casino and still, it feels, not always taken very seriously, the family tragedy seemed terribly cruel."

The article described the family's grief: "Prince Rainier, now fifty-nine years old, his hair white, his face thickened, seemed crushed and numbed. His head hung and when he raised his eyes, tears were on his cheeks. At one point in the funeral ceremony, while a part of Samuel Barber's soaring Adagio for Strings was being played, Prince Albert, who is twenty-four, covered his face in his black-gloved hands. Princess Caroline, who wept, turned toward her father, who sat next to her at the altar, but the prince, partly slumped, eyes half-closed, did not raise his head." The mourners came to this tiny principality, which Grace had put on the map, from the worlds of royalty, show business, and politics. Among them: the Princess of Wales; Nancy Reagan; Danielle Mitterrand, wife of the French President; and film star Cary Grant.

Later, after the mourning family had left the cathedral, a friend of the prince told the *Times* in the same article that the prince was experiencing "one of the most total sadnesses." The friend also said that Stephanie was being confronted with "psychological problems you would not wish on any kid."

Stephanie, still recovering from her injury in the hospital, was unable to attend her mother's funeral. Almost a month later she made her first public appearance after the accident at a memorial service for Princess Grace. Still wearing a neck brace, she appeared shaken and shocked. Though Stephanie was making a rapid physical recovery, she remained emotionally scarred. "She is deeply shaken by her mother's death," a friend of her brother's told *People* magazine at the time. "She hardly talks. She doesn't laugh."

Stephanie managed ultimately to submerge her grief in an outpouring of creative business activities. In her own words: "I was very, very close to my mother. She was my best friend. There were times when I thought it all too difficult. But my mom wouldn't have liked me to just bury my head in my hands and give up. That's not how she brought us up."

CHAPTER 5

The Modeling Caper

IN modeling Stephanie would find, at least for the moment, something to consume her. In a sense such a career choice would be a way to almost jump out of herself and her grief. Modeling, after all, is an external pursuit. But, as things would turn out, Stephanie would be in need of consolation again, this time over the humiliation visited upon her. The American modeling debut of Princess Stephanie turned into one of the most widely publicized no-shows in the history of the fashion industry. Two weeks of photo sessions, press conferences, and parties to launch the "Monaco Mannequin" fell apart at the seams at the eleventh hour. Whether it was a change of heart on Stephanie's part or pressure from the palace, the princess had her tail pulled from the catwalk and was left crying in her Paris apartment two nights before her modeling trip to New York.

Ironically, it was Prince Rainier who pushed her in the direction of fashion. With the mourning period officially over, he insisted that Stephanie begin her studies at the Paris Chamber of Commerce fashion school. At the same time she was spurred on by Marc Bohan of Dior. Years before, as a child, she had been encouraged by fashion designer Vera Maxwell, now in her eighties and retired. "Stephanie designed some fabric for me when she was only fourteen," Maxwell recalls, "and we printed them. She's clever. I think she'll go far. She's got what it takes."

It was not until the spring of 1983 that Stephanie felt strong enough to begin a fashion-design course. Since her mother's death in September of the previous year, she had been in a state of shock, had had crying jags, and had lost weight. But now she was coming out of that period. She enrolled in the $3,000-a-term Ecole de la Chambre Syndicale de la Couture Parisienne. By year's end Dior's Marc Bohan took Stephanie on as a design assistant, a position to which she brought great promise and imagination. She was even given credit for inspiring the design of a languorous collection of 1920s clothes. Bohan was delighted as much by her talent as her personality. "There is a real charm in her and genuine humanity too," Bohan told a colleague, while another co-worker described Stephanie as "original and ready to go." Indeed, everyone seemed happy with Stephanie's progress and talked confidently about her future in the fashion industry.

Then something happened to make those around her think again. By the summer of 1984 Stephanie was turning up at work late. On one occasion she arrived at the *très haute* House of Dior with her hair sprayed bright orange. She was sent home and told to wash it out. The next day she came back with the orange washed out, as instructed, and a new shade, this time green.

Those close to Stephanie at the time attributed her colorful but erratic behavior to her live-in relationship with Paul Belmondo, the son of the actor Jean-Paul Belmondo. The relationship was starting to fall apart. Her moods, they said, hung on the state of their relationship. Sometimes Stephanie even failed to show up for appointments with clients. But Marc Bohan, realizing how valuable a princess could be as a promotional vehicle, did not fire her.

Back at the palace, these antics did not go unnoticed. Her father, Prince Rainier, became increasingly concerned with the behavior of his youngest child and put his foot down. But just as Paul Belmondo seemed to be out of fashion and favor with Stephanie, in came Anthony Delon (son of Alain Delon), along with photos of the two of them that did little to enhance Stephanie's image around the palace. It looked like she might also be dropping her fashion career. She was showing up at trendy Paris nightspots instead of the office. Like last year's collection, Delon was soon to be out of vogue too. Stephanie would replace him with a string of other admirers, as if they were mere fashion accessories.

By January 1985, gone from Dior, Stephanie was now flirting with the idea of a modeling career. As with most of her pursuits, be it careers or men, she brought a single-minded intensity to the modeling. Once again, there would be conflicting reports of what, exactly, was transpiring in this department. And as events would later unfold, nobody could be sure that even Stephanie herself knew the whole story.

What is certain is that Stephanie made the first overture. Paul Hagnauer, who was then director of the leading model agency in Paris, First, remembers meeting Stephanie. "She told me she wanted to become a model," he recalled. "I hired her on the spot." Though she did not possess the looks traditionally associated with a model, nor the experience to match, Hagnauer made no secret of the fact that he was "selling a princess." To be sure, Stephanie could not have picked a profession with a less aristocratic cast.

Princess Stephanie, at five feet eight, is neither very tall nor exceptionally good-looking in the way models are expected to appear. However, the initial reaction to her nascent modeling career got mixed reviews. Gilles Tapie, who photographed her for French *Elle*, commented at the time on Stephanie's unusual look. "She's short for a model," he observed. "She's muscled in the arms and she wears a leather jacket. She could be a boy with her short hair. But when she's in a bathing suit in front of a camera she becomes very feminine." Stephanie, who once had her picture taken in men's underwear, may have been as ambivalent in her own mind about this new career as her looks were androgynous. Her chin, a bit weak, could look like a double chin if photographed from the wrong side. She could also look like a gamine. Her blue-green eyes, the hues of the sea, could be gentle and whimsical as well as stormy and fiery. The effect of her appearance was unpredictable, matching her own individualistic style.

But the princess did get some encouraging responses from the industry, which, no matter how they felt about her, jumped on the royal bandwagon. Industry matriarch Eileen Ford declared that Stephanie was definitely model material. "She's darling, just marvelous looking," Ford, co-founder and secretary of Ford Models, Inc., told an interviewer. "I hadn't noticed that she looked boyish. She has a wonderful figure and a cute alive face. She looks like she's enjoying life, and it's communicated through the camera. She's young and modern looking. If I had her, I'd be a very happy woman."

Karen Hilton, then director of the women's division at Wilhelmina and Stephanie's exclusive agent, was indeed happy. "I think Stephanie is adorable," she was quoted as saying at the time. "Anyone who has visited the most important collections and seen the models on the runway knows that most girls have their heads in the clouds, but Stephanie seemed different. She never struck me as boyish either. People are just looking to say something because she's a princess." Of course, as events transpired on this side of the Atlantic, they would have a lot more to say about the princess. *Vanity Fair* would headline a feature on the no-show American act "Desperately Seeking Stephanie," hinting that this princess might not just be from Monaco, but another planet altogether. On the eve of Stephanie's American trip, Bob Krieger, the legendary international fashion photographer, commented on the chances of a princess-turned-model succeeding: "She has to be extraordinary or nothing at all."

By the time Karen Hilton got the call from Stephanie's Paris agent and friend, Paul Hagnauer, the princess was one of the most sought-after models in the world. Her face had already graced the covers of French *Elle*, Italian *Moda*, and Britain's *Tatler*. Several companies had tried to sign her up. One was Revlon cosmetics. Another was the Click modeling agency in New York whose owner, Frances Grill, told *Vanity Fair*: "Stephanie's family turned down all requests they got from model agencies here. But Stephanie made friends with someone at First in Paris, and First suggested that she go to Wilhelmina. It was a rebellious act against the family's wishes."

Despite her rebel profile, some photographers

found a most cooperative princess. Avi Meroz, the Israeli photographer, for one, was convinced of her professionalism after a two-day photo session. He shot her for the cover of *Moda* magazine. "She was easier than I thought beforehand," he said. "Everybody told me she would be difficult. But she wasn't at all—she was perfect, very professional." Contrary to her reputation for turning up late, as she did on her Dior job, Meroz said that she arrived, sans bodyguards, near the appointed hour. "She got ready quickly," he added, "and she never complained of tiredness. She worked in the same conditions as any other model girl." Others, marveling at Stephanie's unaffected style, observed her snacking on cheese just like them—except for using her fingers instead of a knife and fork.

On the basis of the reports she received from abroad and a previous working relationship with Hagnauer, Wilhelmina's Karen Hilton felt confident about Stephanie's modeling future in America. Just as she would do with any prospective model, Hilton jotted down Stephanie's statistics. "Paul [Hagnauer] gave me the names of the clients she was working with and who was shooting her at the time," Hilton recalls of their first phone conversation regarding Stephanie, "and that she certainly would carry her own weight in terms of what she looked like."

Of Stephanie's style, Hilton said: "Stephanie could look sophisticated dressed up, so to speak, and she could also look like a little cheerleader. In my opinion she had a very androgynous look, which, by the way, is not boyish so much as sexy. At the time Stephanie had short hair, and because of her age and her particular style I could understand why some people would say she kind of looked like a tomboy. But that look was very much in. It could not have been more perfect even if she wasn't a princess."

Nonetheless, the princess factor weighed heavily on the modeling executive's mind. At the time, Hilton had her regular duties supervising sixteen people under her. But owing to Stephanie's royal status and its attendant responsibilities, she said, an extraordinarily detailed plan had to be devised and then approved by Stephanie, Hagnauer, and, presumably, the prince to protect her at every turn.

As such, Hilton made a one-day trip to Paris in March 1985 to meet with her new acquisition. "Because of Stephanie's recognition factor and the magazines she did work for," Hilton remembers thinking, "I felt it was worth making the trip. I knew everybody would pick up on her immediately, which is, of course, what everyone did."

From the outset Hilton had no reservations about a princess-model. Some photographers maintain that famous people—royalty included—do not work well as models. While some observers said that she was not pretty enough, Hilton believed that her look was so interesting and striking that it would become popular among clients. Indeed, Hilton says that, given the chance to represent Princess Diana or Princess Stephanie, she would opt for the model from Monaco. "Princess Diana, in terms of the modeling industry, has a more commercial, tangible kind of look," she explains. "I think if she were not Princess Di, she'd probably be the Miss America pageant type more than she would be a unique blond high-fashion model. But I would say that if Princess Diana wanted to model, she would be able to be successful at it, but more so probably because she's who she is."

The thirty-eight-year-old Hilton, who has spent over twenty years in the industry, allows that Stephanie is not pretty in the same way as Lady Di. "But I personally prefer Stephanie," she says further, "because she has a very definite style and attitude that is different. Because the fashion industry is so competitive, one needs to find separate and different things that are appealing. Not just how someone looks." Almost immediately Hilton discovered how other people were interested in Stephanie. She made some preliminary calls to clients and magazines. "I told people if they were interested to get back to me in five minutes," Hilton reports. "The phones were ringing off the hook."

As a measure of concern, Hilton devoted two weeks, solely and exclusively to devising a launch plan for Stephanie here. "I knew I had to go for the most prestigious," she said. "If you have only ten days, you have to make the trip worthwhile." *Vogue,* for example, would get the fashion exclusive. To ensure this, Hilton had to figure out, if not anticipate, deadlines and how they might be juggled to keep her end of the bargain with each publication. The order in which she thought Stephanie should be published in American magazines was part of the plan. She also had to select one of the morning shows for an appearance by the princess. "It was a matter of balancing and deciding which interviewers Stephanie would feel most comfortable with," Hilton explained. "The same process was used in deciding who should shoot her first."

In search of answers, Hilton flew to Paris. She met Stephanie at the model agency, First, around 10 A.M. on a weekday in March 1985. "Hi ya, cutie," Hilton greeted Stephanie, who replied, "Hi, how ya doing?" This extremely casual and certainly unceremonious exchange, according to Hilton, seemed appropriate. "My first impression of Stephanie," she remembers, "was that she was an adorable kid and she looked like a cheerleader. She had on a pair of cowboy boots, jeans, and a football jacket. She spoke just like an American kid who was a cheerleader. I did not detect any accent whatsoever."

Still, it was clear to Hilton that there was a difference. "Stephanie seemed quite contained, quite comfortable," the modeling director observed. "I think that twenty-year-old kids can be uneasy with themselves sometimes. And then you take a twenty-one-year-old kid who is a princess and has had a rather eventful, extended adolescent life and there you have Stephanie."

Throughout their day together Hilton would be struck by the duality of Stephanie's existence. Often she would do a double take as a result. On the way to lunch, with Stephanie and Hagnauer, she noticed a woman who looked to be in her nineties and some grade school children in uniforms stop in their tracks at recognizing Stephanie. "Stephanie hopped in her little car, just like a teenager would do," Hilton said. "And she drove like everybody in Paris drives. But it also dawned on me what she must go through and what she is subjected to all the time."

Stephanie selected a restaurant where they knew her. "The maître d', who was probably in his late twenties, took our order," Hilton recalls. "I'm sure Stephanie frequented the place, because they were like old chums." Over salad and salmon, they discussed the plan Hilton had drawn up for her. Stephanie read it over quickly. "I found her to be quite strong, quite opinionated," says Hilton. "She went down the list of events and said, 'This one I want to do, this one we'll talk about, this one is no problem, this one looks good to me.' "

One aspect of the plan evoked an especially strong

reaction. It was the prospect of a press conference. "As far as Stephanie was concerned," Hilton recounts, "a press conference really did not have anything to do with her coming to New York and modeling. Most of the time she assumed that she would be subjected to questions about her mother. She was not in New York to have a press conference about her mom; she was there to do modeling assignments. So if I could hold the press to asking her questions about modeling exclusively, then she would agree to do a press conference in an environment where she was protected."

Such protection, according to the plan, would mean that Stephanie would arrive and leave without interference. "I would be standing next to her," Hilton explains further, "taking the questions and allowing her to answer questions that were pertinent and avoiding those that were not."

Reflecting on Stephanie's instructions, Hilton says: "She appeared to me to be a very strong-willed girl who had her own opinions and wanted to make all her own decisions. I think that after a number of years have passed and you've been in the limelight, to a degree because of a tragedy like her mother's death, that you learn to handle the conversation which is, 'I'm there to be a model. I am not there to answer questions about my mother because that's what they [the press] love to ask me and that's not what I'm doing now.'"

Stephanie, according to plan, would be protected from the moment she set foot on American soil. Scheduled to arrive on a Sunday, she would be whisked from an Air France jet into a limousine waiting for her on the tarmac. No one would know her time of arrival in order to avoid a press stampede at the airport. Morgans, a chic hotel on Madison Avenue in the Thirties, owned by former Studio 54 disco owners Steve Rubell and Ian Schrager, would be her temporary home. Its contemporary look, very high-tech with dramatic black and white checked bathrooms, and a young, friendly staff in designer uniforms without the usual cardboardlike material and stiff braiding, attract celebrities like Farrah Fawcett, Tina Turner, Bianca Jagger, Cher, and the Hollywood brat pack featuring Timothy Hutton and Rob Lowe, an ex-beau of Stephanie's.

But the 154-room Morgans' style and comfort were not the only reasons for Stephanie being booked in there. Hilton's apartment was a block and a half away and thus she could look after Stephanie. Wilhelmina's Hilton also knew and trusted that Rubell, with whom she discussed the arrangements, understood the potential for a massive invasion of Stephanie's privacy and could guarantee that this would not occur. Hilton also arranged for two professional bodyguards to accompany her everywhere. They would be posted outside the duplex penthouse, in which Stephanie was to stay, and take their rest periods in two adjoining bedrooms.

Despite these elaborate security precautions, the princess-model would not feel too enclosed in this space. The duplex penthouse features a master bedroom, bathroom, and office on the first floor. A wooden spiral staircase would lead Stephanie to a living room, dining room, bathroom, kitchen, and two terraces. The view was as close as anyone could get to the Empire State Building without taking a tour of it.

This seemingly fail-safe plan, however, hinged on the prince's approval. The princess skipped over this detail. But Hilton assumed that Paris agent Hagnauer had already worked that out because by then Stephanie had been photographed for European magazines. Of course, it was expected that the plan would be shown to the prince as a matter of protocol. "Let's go for it," Stephanie told Hilton, who remarks, "It seemed to me that New York was quite important to her because it was part of her plan to be a model."

Back at the agency they hammered out further details of Stephanie's whirlwind American modeling tour. There they were joined by Stephanie's German shepherd puppy, Atmo, whom the princess picked up at her apartment on the way back. During the meeting Stephanie played with the puppy. "She kind of wrestled on the floor with the puppy," Hilton remembers. "They played like kids. The dog was really like her little friend. I mean, she adored the dog and showed him an enormous amount of affection. She takes the dog everywhere. I was very impressed with the way she looks after her dog."

Stephanie would be booked solid every day. Denis Piel was to photograph her for *Vogue. Entertainment Tonight* would film the session for television. *Life* enlisted Patrick Demarchelier to photograph Stephanie. ABC would cover that one. *Rolling Stone* planned to make her a cover girl. The late Bill King was set to photograph a *Mademoiselle* cover. The *Today* show would tape that session and also interview the princess. "I explained that she would have a very tight schedule," Hilton says, "so Stephanie knew this was a serious plan." On Monday alone, the day after her arrival, Stephanie would appear on a morning television program, give a short press conference, and attend a black-tie dinner in her honor.

The dinner was to be held at Le Club, a private club off New York's Sutton Place, that a decade before had been quite tony and international. Now it was something of a dowager on the disco scene. Nonetheless, around eighty guests, including the most important fashion designers of the day, were expected. Clearly, the press was excluded. In addition to selecting the flowers—a pink and pale green —herself, Hilton also arranged for invitations to be hand-delivered at the last minute in order to hide the location from the paparazzi sure to turn up outside and converge on Stephanie. "The details that were involved in working with somebody like Stephanie were amazing even to me," Hilton says with a sigh. "I'd worked with some very famous models before. But here you had to be concerned not only with every single minute of the day, but also with the possibilities of what could occur every single minute of the day. And at the same time you had to be sure that Stephanie was comfortable."

All that was missing was a contract for Stephanie to sign. A verbal agreement would do for the moment. The princess said that the fees, ranging from $5,000 to $10,000 a day, were acceptable to her. Each fee, according to Hilton, would depend on who the client was, and what they wanted to do with her. "It was a matter of just giving the information to Stephanie," she explains, "and her saying okay. I had gotten Stephanie fees that were acceptable to her, from magazines, designers, and clients."

The rather informal meeting in Paris continued until dark, with Hilton and Hagnauer attending a concert with Stephanie. They stopped briefly at Stephanie's small one-bedroom apartment and stayed just long enough for Karen Hilton to have a look around. Hilton remembers: "It wasn't a mess. Nor was it necessarily neat and tidy like I would have with a family. There might have been a sweatshirt on the couch. You know, stuff like that. The apartment was modern with a bare wood floor. It was light. She had a lot of knickknacks, especially frogs, around." Hilton adds, "Her dog was running around. Stephanie did her farewells. She gave him kisses and told him to behave and that she'd be back later."

Hilton, originally scheduled to fly back to New York that night, figured it was worthwhile to spend more time in the princess's company. After all, Stephanie would be under exclusive contract with her in America. At the concert, the modeling executive had another insight into what was involved with protecting Stephanie's privacy. They had to enter the auditorium by a special doorway and be escorted to their seats in the second or third row. In no time Stephanie's presence attracted attention from others in the audience as well as photographers trying to get close enough to take her picture. "I think there's always a moment when Stephanie decides whether she's going to be cute and entertaining," Hilton surmises, "or whether she is going to tell them not to do that."

It was then that Hilton got her first lesson in handling the princess and the press. "I just reached over and touched her hand and smiled and told her, 'It's okay, just smile and talk to me, and we'll be involved in a conversation," Hilton recounts. "They took a couple of photos and then I nodded to them, as if to say 'That's enough, guys,' and they moved away with a lot of respect. They thanked Stephanie and she sort of nodded—'that's okay.' Then the concert began."

That circumstance alerted Hilton once again to the royal conflict inside Stephanie, about which they had had a discussion earlier that day. " 'Everybody would like to bounce into New York and have a good time,'" Hilton remembers telling the princess-model. " 'But we have to remember, honey, that you're a princess. That's your lot in life. That's what you are. So we need to respect that and pay attention to that. I will take care of all the peripheral parts that will come up because you are a princess, but we need to remember that that's what you are.' " To which, according to the worldly modeling executive, Stephanie sighed and said, "I know."

At the concert Stephanie behaved like any normal twenty-year-old. "She tapped her foot when the songs got faster," Hilton says. "She wasn't acting outrageous or sitting there quietly either, but just behaving like most people." She played the part of a princess only after the show by getting backstage for a brief visit with the singer.

After the concert they all repaired to Hagnauer's apartment for dinner. By now it was nearly 10:30 P.M., a little over twelve hours since Hilton had first met Princess Stephanie. There were about six to eight other people there. "It was very casual," Hilton recalls, "with people sitting around with their legs over the chair having coffee and dessert. Then we hung out in the living room afterward for a while. Stephanie got neither more nor less attention than anyone else."

Confident that things were rolling right along, Hilton flew home the next morning on the Concorde. Back in the office she began drafting the final plan as agreed upon by Hagnauer and Stephanie. Within days of arriving back in New York, Hilton received a call from Frank Cresci, Monaco's consul in America, about Stephanie's modeling scheme. She was not surprised. "Stephanie had talked about him," Hilton says. "She adores the man. I believe he's a long-time family friend. He's known Stephanie since she was a baby. Stephanie said that she wanted me to meet him because, in any event, he would want to meet me. It was certainly a request by her father, too, that we meet."

They met for breakfast. "It became apparent that he was very concerned," Hilton recalls. "I did not ask him to go into his concerns. I had already taken care of protocol and security details as best I could on my end. What remained to be done in this area was a matter between him and the prince. Everything that might worry him I had already cleared up." Cresci said that should the prince approve the plans, he wanted to meet the princess at the airport.

Cresci, a former New York City cop assigned to the special investigative unit, met the Grimaldis while assigned to escort Princess Grace while she was in town. Later Rainier took him on as consul. After the Cresci meeting, Hilton assumed that things were proceeding as planned. Any further details regarding Rainier's approval, it was understood by Hilton, would be handled by Hagnauer back in Paris. Telexes went back and forth between Stephanie's American and Parisian agents the week before she was to arrive in New York. The plan seemed to have the approval of the prince.

On the Friday prior to Stephanie's arrival on Sunday, Hilton was relaxing in her office for the first time in nearly one month. Over the last two weeks alone she had put in fourteen-hour days to ensure that Stephanie's modeling debut in America would be a success. "I was in my office at the very end of the day," she remembers, "and thinking, 'Okay, we've made it this far.'"

Hilton's peace of mind was interrupted by the phone ringing. It was exactly five o'clock, New York time. She picked it up and could not believe at first what she was hearing. In short, Princess Stephanie would not be arriving in New York on Sunday, as planned, because her father had canceled the trip and was forbidding her to go to New York. The call was from one of the new owners, a Swiss woman, of First, the Paris agency where Hagnauer was the director. "This is impossible," Hilton told her. "This cannot be happening. I'll need an explanation as to why."

What she got amounted to a royal edict. Herewith, according to Hilton, the exact explanation she got: "Mr. Hagnauer has given you all the wrong information and he should never have approved this trip. Stephanie didn't have the right to approve this trip because she's not twenty-one years old. Her father is preventing her from leaving the country at this time. He does not want her to go to New York with Mr. Hagnauer. And that's it—there is nothing you can do." Hilton dashed off a telegram to the palace in Monaco and its Paris Embassy as well, both to no avail. By then it was eleven o'clock Paris time, and to this day Hilton says that she cannot be sure her missives ever reached Rainier. There was no reply. She went home and rang up Hagnauer, whom she describes as "a very upscale guy, a gentleman," with whom she'd had excellent dealings in the past. She discovered that he had been fired. "He was horribly embarrassed," Hilton said. "Obviously the new owners had the ear of someone at the palace and convinced them that Paul was an idiot." She theorizes that the Avi Meroz pictures, which appeared in *Moda* prior to the trip, bolstered the new owners' campaign to destroy Hagnauer's credibility. Stephanie posed with a cigarette and a beer can in her hand. Photographer Meroz allowed in a *Time* interview that *Moda* "did too much, too soon" with his pictures. "They tried to make her special and, in a way, I wanted that too, but the way they did the pages Stephanie came out as a shock."

Hilton waited until Saturday to call Stephanie. "Never mind that she's got modeling assignments," Hilton remembers thinking. "I'm going to call and make sure Stephanie is okay." Hagnauer, who had been back and forth on the phone all day and night with her, told Hilton that the princess was very upset. "When Stephanie picked up the phone," Hilton recalls, "she was very upset—crying—and was on the other phone with her father. She said, 'I'm on the phone. I can't really talk. I'll have to call you back.'"

To this day she has never called back. But Hilton feels no anger or bitterness toward the princess. "Poor Stephanie," Hilton says, "had gotten into the middle of an argument that was really between two business people at a modeling agency, and she was once again being pulled in two or three different directions." Six months later First, the agency, folded. Hilton, today managing director of an avant-garde Tribeca modeling agency, BethAnn, and also the representative of an American Impressionist painter, still believes that Stephanie was completely honorable about her intentions. "She was professional and cooperative," Hilton insists. "Stephanie wanted to be a model. I thought that I could make that possible for her."

The official line that Hilton put out to the press: "Stephanie's father did not want her to come to New York and the reasons were not really explained."

That explanation did nothing to quiet the speculation about Stephanie's mental state. Shortly after her due date in New York, the princess was hospitalized at the Belvedere Clinic in Paris. Though the institute specializes in gynecological problems, her stay there fueled rumors about exhaustion. The official palace explanation was influenza.

Despite negative reactions to the episode, there were many people who thought well of Stephanie. One was photographer Bill King, who had photographed her in Europe for *Vanity Fair.* "She's really lovely to work with," he remarked after her aborted American debut. "I would love to see Stephanie again," Hilton says. "Not to discuss this, but just as a person whom I happened to think was quite adorable. I think Stephanie creates a feeling in people of wanting to protect her."

Wilhelmina's president, William Weinberg, does not feel similarly. "If I am going to be truthful," he says, "I am going to put her in a very bad light. We organized her schedules and had a nice welcoming party arranged, but she didn't show up." He adds: "We never received an apology."

In the end Princess Stephanie would protect her father's image. One news report had him reading the paternal riot act, which left Stephanie shaken and unhappy. Honoring his wishes and realizing, perhaps, her own misgivings about a modeling career, Stephanie would later explain about her decision: "I never would have done it if he'd said, 'I don't want you to model.' But he didn't."

CHAPTER 6

Stephanie the Businesswoman

IT was in November 1984 that Stephanie, dreaming about a holiday in Mauritius, came up with the idea for her own business. Unable to find a swimsuit to her liking, Stephanie sketched her own design and showed it to her best friend and colleague, Alix de la Comble, at Dior. "Marvelous," said Alix, "let's make it ourselves." As Alix remembers, "We sat in the same room for three months before we spoke. Then, one day, we both started trying on designer shoes and began laughing like a couple of children. From then on we were friends. We decided to do something in swimwear. So we took a gamble, quit our jobs, and we won."

Initially the Grimaldi name did not prompt any special business treatment. "Nobody helped us with financing or gave us advice. We had to look up in the phone book to find out who made bathing suits because we didn't know anything." Further, Stephanie's royal position seemed more a hindrance than a help. "People don't expect to see somebody like me walk into an office and say, 'We need a loan for a company to make bathing suits.' " Though allowing that a princess might get more publicity than most swimsuit designers, Stephanie was also well aware that the highly competitive fashion industry would be more interested in profits than titles. After all, how many royals are successful in retail?

"Buyers aren't stupid," said Stephanie. "They're not going to buy anything they can't sell—especially not at royal prices." Her designs carried a much higher price tag than other bathing costumes. But despite the odds the two girls, after hours of careful planning, decided to take the plunge. "We wanted to show people in fashion that two young girls with an idea in their heads can be very professional," she vowed, "even if they are young. In France nobody believes that young people can do anything. It's incredible. But we had to get out there." To finance this venture they borrowed money from their brothers, added whatever they could scrape up themselves, and counted a meager 180,000 francs ($29,000). Now, with enough money to keep them in croissants and thread, they set up a one-room shop. Atmo, Stephanie's German shepherd puppy, kept them company.

"We began to dream of going places," Alix said, and Stephanie chimed in, "To the beaches." They drew inspiration from their own tastes. The bathing suits would reflect a happy, upbeat, sensual Mediterranean temperament. Suprisingly, for someone who had been constantly photographed in bikinis, she came up with a one-piece swimsuit. It would be the last thing most people would expect from this princess. But her reasoning was quite practical. "I've lived by the sea for over twenty years," she explained, "without ever managing to find shops with swimsuits that please me." Brigitte Bardot made bi-

The home of Caroline and Stephanie—the Palace.
MONACO TOURIST OFFICE

The harbor—Monaco.
MONACO TOURIST OFFICE

A very serious student: Princess Caroline during her exams at the Palace, 1964. WIDE WORLD PHOTOS

Princess Grace and Stephanie with Fred Astaire, 1967.
WIDE WORLD PHOTOS

Meilleurs vœux
de Joyeux Noël
et d'Heureuse Année
1982

Grace

The Grimaldi family Christmas card.
PROVIDED BY FATHER PETER JACOBS

Stephanie after her release from the hospital, following her stay for injuries sustained in the car accident that killed her mother. WIDE WORLD PHOTOS

The picture tells the story—a family stricken with grief.
WIDE WORLD PHOTOS

Families from two of the world's most popular soap operas unite: the Carringtons and the Grimaldis. WIDE WORLD PHOTOS

Princess Stephanie at a gala at Harrod's, London.
REX FEATURES

Stephanie with her latest beau, Mario Oliver, at the French
Open Tennis Championships, 1987. WIDE WORLD PHOTOS

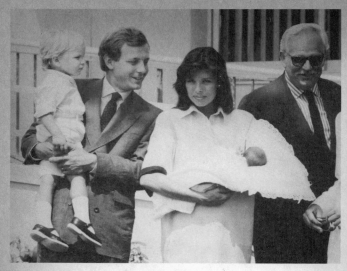

The second time around—Caroline with her second husband Stefano Casiraghi and their children, son, Andrea, and newborn Charlotte Marie. WIDE WORLD PHOTOS

kinis popular some three decades before and since then one-piece suits have seldom been in vogue on the Côte d'Azur.

Drawing once again on personal experience, Stephanie came up with the name Pool Position for their company. The name is a play on Pole Position, the Grimaldis' observation point for the world-famous Monaco Grand Prix which their tiny country hosts each year. Right from the start, Stephanie's vision was clear: "A swimsuit that was sexy, but not vulgar." The collection also included skirts, pants, and robes made of a sheer nylon/Lycra, a stretch fabric. "I make clothes that can be worn all day to the beach," she added, "and then to go out to dinner in the evening."

Clearly the sleek swimwear was not made with royalty in mind. "I am a princess of the twentieth century," Stephanie explained. "Of course I have to dress suitably for official functions, but what I wear in private is my affair." Her one-piece maillots, with deep plunges in the front and high rises in the back, certainly would not travel well at charity events. Further, the swimsuits did not require the kind of anorectic bodies that turn up at such affairs. "You can be a little chubby," Stephanie allowed mischievously.

Stephanie and her partner, Alix, decided on an official launch of the collection in Monaco. Despite her own success, however brief and curtailed, as a model, a trim and fit princess hired others to do the job. Stephanie kicked off the event with an upbeat "get-set-go" to the models who then slid down into the swimming pool.

"She's a kind of sporty version of Madonna," said Karl Lagerfeld, the celebrated fashion designer who makes his home in Monaco, and one of 260 intimates who attended the spirited, joke-filled poolside launch of her swimwear collection. "She designs bathing suits the way Chanel designed her little Chanel suits. She knows exactly what she wants and they're very well done." Another person in the audience observed, "Just like what the princess wears in real life —sporty, very colorful, modern and chic." In a splash of celebration the princess and Alix jumped in the pool. The "little fish," as Stephanie was nicknamed as a little girl, said that if she were an animal she would be a dolphin.

Her biggest fan—much to Princess Stephanie's delight—was her father. This time, unlike the modeling episode, there were no problems for the princess. Instead Rainier reacted by hugging Stephanie as she pulled herself up and out of the pool. As Stephanie recalls, "He was very unsure about the swimsuits to start, but he was pleased that I was going to make a success of it." Her brother, Albert, and sister, Caroline, also congratulated their baby sister.

Soon Stephanie and Alix shared not only a thriving business, but also an apartment in the sixteenth arrondissement, an upscale district of Paris. Alix would also become a close friend of the Grimaldi family, socializing with them and on occasion traveling with them as well. Describing their collaboration, Alix, who had been a Dior trainee specializing in wedding gowns, said, "She was ten years younger than me so I designed the more sophisticated look and she did the younger, more plunging style. The partnership worked very well." Later she would marry someone whom she met through Stephanie and also sell out her interest in Pool Position to the princess, who, at work, was "just plain Stephanie Grimaldi."

Their swimwear business flourished far beyond the principality. In England and America it was a huge success. Stephanie and Alix traveled together to

America to launch the collection in Atlanta. Rich's, a local department-store chain there, had purchased the right to introduce the line in America. The bid was a reported $500,000. *The Washington Post*'s coverage of her store visit indicated that it was big local attraction. Hundreds of people turned up with varying motives. One man came all the way from Los Angeles, where Stephanie would later do a West Coast launch, because, he said, "She's royalty and she's tall." Another man, with the same surname of Grimaldi, turned up in the hope they might be related. There was one disgruntled customer, among many who begged for autographs, who walked off muttering, "I thought *she* was going to model the swimsuits."

The question on the minds of many people in attendance was, Why does this youngest member of one of Europe's most respectable families want to do this? "I've always been interested in clothes from as early as I can remember," says the princess who unashamedly prefers blue jeans to ball gowns. "I used to love playing paper dolls with my mother. She would cut them, and I would dress them." After the Rich's presentation of the collection, attended by loud applause, fans moved closer to get a look at the young princess. "I've seen every one of her mother's films," said one. "If she comes from Grace Kelly, then that's good enough for me." A sixteen-year-old boy, who skipped school with some of his friends, explained her appeal. "I read her father didn't want her to become a model, but she's doing it anyway. She's a rebel. Wish we could do that, but we're not as brave."

Indeed, her bravery in starting over—instead of sulking over the modeling ban—paid off. Bloomingdale's and Macy's quickly bought her swimwear in America as did Harrod's in London. In less than a year the company boasted sales of 28,000 items, in the $80 to $150 range. In one twenty-four-hour period, Rich's recorded sales of twenty swimsuits, twelve of them retailing at $124 each.

The success of Pool Position, according to one of the top swimsuit manufacturers in Los Angeles, was due not to her title, but her talent. "The woman must want to buy it and wear it and have it look good on her body," the swimwear manufacturer said. "If it doesn't fit, then I don't care whose name is on it. It won't sell." Confident that that would not be the case with the majority of women, Stephanie pulled off a major business triumph with Pool Position. As far as the princess knew, only one person close to her could not buy one of her suits. This was her sister, Caroline. "She'll be so pregnant that the suits won't stretch enough," Stephanie said, adding, "Maybe we'll make one special for her."

Emboldened by her success, the princess now felt anything was possible. Pool Position had been set up by Stephanie and Alix. Without the help of her family, Stephanie had managed, through her own talents and on her own terms, to make it work. Having risen phoenixlike from scorching press notices about her short-lived modeling career, the princess knew that from now on, nobody or nothing would keep her from achieving whatever goal she set for herself.

Princess Stephanie did not tread water for too long, but plunged right into yet another career. This time serendipity played a part. The same evening that she was dining out with some friends at a Paris restaurant, one of France's leading record producers was at a table nearby. Stephanie was introduced to him.

His name was Yves Roze. As the evening progressed, Yves invited her to make a record. Instead of doodling on a tablecloth the princess ended up signing her name to a contract that he had scribbled on it. "I thought it was a joke," she later admitted, her green eyes still registering surprise. "People make all kinds of silly proposals when they meet a princess."

Forty-eight hours later the princess realized this was no joke. She found herself in a Paris recording studio doing voice tests. Despite her nervousness, Roze still thought she had tremendous potential. Though some critics later described her voice as "tinny" or "bubblegum," Roze acted on his instinct. At the same time, Roze recognized her limitations as well. To this end he searched for a simple tune, one that could be recorded quickly and would not be too ambitious for someone who had never sung professionally before. Instead of going with a cover version of a hit tune, often a safe bet, Roze turned to a songwriter to come up with an original tune. Jack Robinson, an Englishman, was that person. He came up with a song called "Irresistible," a title that matched the appeal of this princess as well. Stephanie was delighted by the end product: "Jack Robinson did a great job with the words."

The sentiments conveyed by the song made it seem like Stephanie could have thought them up herself. She sang the song in French on the "A" side, and in English on the back. It went, in the English translation, "He's in my system though I try and resist him. I can't fight him anymore. Irresistible. I can't fight him anymore. Irresistible. I can't find the temptation. Call it physical. Call it logical, still I want the sensation."

The record would surface as number one in France. But the sharks were out there once again. This time, instead of criticizing her appearance, they sniped at her sound—going so far as to suggest that the voice on the record belonged to someone else. "That just stimulated me to do better," Stephanie recalls. "When I designed my swimsuit collection, people said, 'Oh, it's easy for her.' Well, I'm sorry, but it wasn't easy. Just because I was born a princess doesn't mean that I was born with every talent in the world."

Everywhere she went on a huge media campaign to promote the record, people were still asking, as they did with her modeling and swimwear designing before, *why* is the princess doing this? Whereas she was mum, if not also muzzled, on the aborted modeling career, this time Stephanie spoke out. "I wanted to show everyone I could do it," she would tell her inquisitors, "and I also wanted to prove to myself that I could sing. I couldn't just sit around and do nothing. That's not how we were brought up." Then, much to her own amazement, she added, "Who would think that *I* could sing?"

The pop princess was also quick to point out all the work she put into her new career. "I worked very hard in the studio," she said. "Then I'd practice on my own for hours." Working closely with her producer and sound technicians, she said that she supervised every last detail. Of her co-workers, Stephanie declared, "They wanted to get the finest results. How could I treat such enthusiasm lightly?" They worked what seemed like interminable hours over four months. "I didn't want anyone to say that I was getting by on my name," Stephanie remarked.

Indeed, had Stephanie only been interested in the trappings of a rock star, it would probably have been easy for her either to date or marry one. But diligent work, not osmosis, was her favored method of operating in this arena. Not one to play second fiddle to anyone else, Stephanie wanted achievements she could call her own. "It wasn't just a fight for recognition or fame," a close associate explains. "She had fame. She was a public figure the day she was born. She didn't ask for it. She didn't fight for it in the way an actor or singer or writer will. She wanted something in a sense that was purer than fame. She wanted achievement, self-respect. And she had the drive, the guts, the passion, to get exactly what she wanted." A totally unaffected princess, she said, "Just call me Stephanie," when she was interviewed by this author (Crimp) at the time. She put out Atmo, her German shepherd, who was making the reporter uncomfortable. "She chainsmoked, laughed, joked, and put us on equal footing. No snobbery or protocol."

Risking all manner of public humiliation by cutting a record with no prior experience or voice training, the princess said she knew she could pull it off. "I wouldn't want to waste professionals' time," she said. "I am not like that. It wouldn't be respectful. I wanted to sing, and that's why I made the record. I just wanted people to dance to it and enjoy it."

Indeed, Stephanie saw her wish come true. "Irresistible" had "hurricane" (its French translation) sales, 1.3 million copies in Europe in just three months. By comparison, Madonna's "Like a Virgin" did only 400,000 sales on the Continent. "Hurricane" stood at the top of the French charts for over six weeks.

Producer Roze heaped praise on the pop-singing princess. "Stephanie is an absolute dream to work with. You can't get away with a thing. She's amazing. She would put in a twelve-hour stint on the album and still go out to dinner looking as fresh as if she had just started her day. Her leftover energy could light a small town."

Monégasques also beamed with pride. The tiny principality, until now, had only played host to—never spawned—a pop star. While their initial reaction to Grace Kelly the Hollywood movie star was one of skepticism, they seemed comfortable with their homegrown star. What's more, the princess donated her royalties from her hit record to the Princess Grace Foundation to benefit struggling young artists.

Once again Stephanie proved to be a savvy businesswoman. Normally a singer earns around 7 percent from the sales of a record, but the princess had negotiated a 14 percent royalty. After all, who would know more about a "royalty" than Stephanie?

Strange though it may have appeared at the time, Stephanie's music career was not that much of a break from family tradition. Her mother, Grace Kelly, had recorded "True Love" with Bing Crosby from the movie *High Society*. On the record cover Stephanie, cool and serene in white, looks as soft and elegant as her mother. Once again, Grace's girl Stephanie would reflect her creative spirit.

CHAPTER 7

Royal Romances

JUST as interest in Caroline's divorce subsided, the tabloid press began to point their poison pens at Stephanie. Her dalliances with some of the world's most attractive yet sometimes royally unsuitable men landed her in the headlines. The same direction and discipline she brought to her successful international ventures would not always characterize her romances.

By the summer of 1981, long before her mother's tragic death, the princess had been linked with a succession of young men. Among them were Miguel Bose, the son of one of Spain's most famous bullfighters, Luis-Miguel Dominguin; Ted Kennedy, Jr., a member of America's most celebrated political dynasty; and Italian socialite Duke Urbano Riario Sforza Barberini Colonna. But they seemed to be nothing more serious than crushes. Without such a public profile, of course, Stephanie would have been viewed as just a normal young woman with a string of limited-run romances. The inventions of the press were matched only by Stephanie's fantasy of her ideal man, which she shared with a French magazine. The dream sequence has the princess stuck in traffic when, suddenly, her car is hit by another. "I am furious and I get out ready to yell," she relates. "The man who crashed into me gets out of his car just as annoyed as me. He's around thirty years old, tall, brown-haired, with sunglasses, wearing a T-shirt, and he beams. It's love at first sight for both of us."

Next, as the fantasy evolves, they exchange telephone numbers. "He calls me the same day," Stephanie continues, "and we decide to have dinner together. We choose a small restaurant, quiet and friendly. He comes to pick me up in his dented car. On the way we both get stuck in traffic. We both start laughing. He leans toward me and kisses me."

In real life, however, things have not turned out quite that simply for her. Her first true love was Paul Belmondo. Central casting could not have come up with a more perfect couple. Here was Paul, the handsome, athletic son of France's most famous actor, Jean-Paul Belmondo, and Stephanie, daughter of a Hollywood actress-turned-princess. It looked like the stuff of which fairy-tale love stories are made. The couple met in the posh Paris private club Elysées-Matignon in October 1981. Sixteen at the time, she fell madly in love. Her love for the seventeen-year-old Belmondo bordered on the obsessive. Grace feared that Stephanie would neglect her studies to service this passion day and night. Under her mother's watchful eye, Stephanie managed to summon the concentration to pass her baccalauréat in the spring of 1982. Grace did not want her daughter's talent spent completely on her emotions. Stephanie, who had shown talent as early as fourteen at drawing and design, had an opportunity to apprentice with Dior's Marc Bohan. For Stephanie that meant being in Paris and close to Paul. Above all, would Stephanie, loved so unequivocally her whole childhood, have the emotional cushion to protect her feelings?

To this end Grace and Rainier remanded Stephanie to Monaco and Roc Agel for the summer of 1982. This dictum created friction between mother and daughter. It was not a question of the Grimaldis not liking Belmondo, but more a matter of helping a lovesick Stephanie to slow down. So great was her ardor that she needed to put a brake on her emotions. Grace and Rainier did not want their obviously gifted baby daughter to make a career out of being in love. Much as they liked and approved of Belmondo, the Grimaldis realized their daughter was too young to marry. Grace, who had given up a career as an actress, also did not want Stephanie to surrender her talents to marriage before she had a chance to explore them. The Grimaldis feared that Stephanie's relentless passion might overwhelm Belmondo's common sense and the two of them might elope.

As events would unfold, Belmondo would appear at Stephanie's side not at the altar, but during the saddest moment of her life in September. Upon hearing of her mother's death, Belmondo immediately jumped in his car and drove all the way from Paris to Monaco to be at Stephanie's side at the hospital. Indeed, many close to both of them attribute Stephanie's recovery from her bereavement to their union. "He seems to be the only one who can make her laugh," Rainier told friends, adding, "Paul is a charming boy and very attentive to Stephanie. The two get on perfectly."

Rainier took a liking to the young man whose behavior bespoke a certain maturity. Though Belmondo, like Stephanie, had little interest in academics, he brought enormous discipline to a motor-racing career. His living habits were clean and ordered. Instead of hanging around clubs and drinking until the wee hours of the morning, Belmondo got up early each day and abstained from alcohol. Of his ambitions, Belmondo would say: "If you don't dream a little, it's rather sad. You should always want something you can't have. It gives you a goal."

Belmondo was considered a delight. Described by friends as courteous and discreet, he appeared to be exactly the right match for a young princess. Life in the fast lane of motor-racing did not alter his essentially polite personality. Despite his tempered ways, Belmondo was no dullard. Very much his father's son, Paul enjoyed physical risk (Jean-Paul never let stuntmen stand in for him in films) as well as beautiful women. Paul had learned on his father's knee to drive. His rich and famous father was not the only distinguished member of the Belmondo family. Paul's grandfather was one of France's most eminent sculptors. As such, Paul, much like Stephanie, grew up in the public eye. They also shared an Anglo-French upbringing. Belmondo, born in Paris, had lived in both England and France.

In love, though, Paul and Stephanie acted much the same as any other teenagers. In Paris, Paul would pick Stephanie up from school for a lunch date. Back in Monaco they might share an innocent teenage embrace during a tennis tournament. Of course, there was always a crowd, namely the press, to intrude on and somehow taint these sweet moments. During this period Paul was overheard saying, "That's the disadvantage of being known and being with someone who is known. Photographers follow us wherever we go." But instead of despairing over the situation, Paul was determined that his relationship would not be damaged by so much unwanted publicity. "The less people talk about relationships with Stephanie," Belmondo vowed, "the better it will be. I live by the philosophy that ultimately you can get what you want."

Or so he thought. Alas, if Stephanie was what Paul really wanted, he was doomed to be disappointed. Though the press was marrying them off, the princess had another agenda, one that did not feature Belmondo, though he had played such a soothing role during her recovery from the car crash that took her mother's life. Emerging from the long shadow of grief, Stephanie was ready for some fun again in her life. To her thinking, Belmondo's sense of adventure was limited to the race course, and socially he was rather dull. The fast lane for the princess was the disco, not the Grand Prix, circuit where she would dance the night away with the international jet set. Paul, on the other hand, was more of a homebody with his habit of turning in early.

In this environment, Stephanie landed next in the arms of Anthony Delon, also the son of an actor, Alain Delon. But the similarity between Alain and Paul stopped there. Delon junior, who possessed the good looks of his father, was considered by those who knew him to be something of a street-smart delinquent. At nineteen, he also had quite a track record with women. Stephanie, by all accounts, found him irresistible. As she would tell a colleague from Dior, "You can't imagine how bored I've been these last two years. How I've prayed for excitement. Now the chance has come. I intend to grab it with both hands."

Stephanie's enthusiasm was as much a betrayal as a rebuke to Paul. Her new attachment escalated a rivalry that had existed between Belmondo and Delon. From the time the two virile young men knew of each other, they competed for the title of "France's He-man." To be Stephanie's boyfriend would bring either one of them a notch closer to the title. In the end Belmondo would exhibit an emotional strength. Anthony's victory in winning Stephanie's affections did not cause Paul too many sleepless nights. Not long after her departure from his life, Belmondo reflected, "When I was involved with Stephanie it happened naturally. I never looked at it as if I were being used. But now with some distance, I see how you can lose your private life. I would never repeat this. It's enough to make you pity the poor princess."

Delon, on the other hand, seemed to covet the limelight. His reputation as a lady-killer could only garner publicity for his budding business as a leatherjacket manufacturer. Delon, according to friends, liked to be seen at all the in places and then to read about it in the right columns.

They had first met, actually, on Stephanie's seventeenth birthday. By then the princess was already smitten with Belmondo. But apparently Delon had ignited some interest on her part. At a Paris club the princess and Anthony seemed to hit it off instantly and spent much of the evening whispering in each other's ears. Delon drove Stephanie back to the Grimaldis' apartment. She never heard from him again, and gave little thought to this as she was already committed to Belmondo.

Then came the summer of 1984. Stephanie was in Monaco, and so, too, was Anthony. The paparazzi were not far behind. They caught the two of them embracing on the beach. Belmondo, meanwhile, was reportedly spending a few days with his mother elsewhere in France. Belmondo told friends at the time that Stephanie was phoning him constantly. His plan was to go to Monaco to be with her. Belmondo never made the trip.

The princess had rung up again, this time to inform Belmondo of the photographs. Someone who overheard the conversation from Paul's end reported that they both yelled a lot at each other. Paul, by then furious, said it was finished between them. Thus ended the puppy love between the so-called perfect partners.

Delon would get the same royal snub as Caroline's ex-husband, Philippe Junot. Anthony's background was cause for concern at the palace in Monaco. Born in Los Angeles, he divided his time between his parents after their divorce. Something of an indifferent student, Delon junior did not pass his baccalauréat. By an early age he had developed a taste for nightlife and in his wanderings fell in with some less than savory characters. In January 1983, police stopped Anthony and a friend in a stolen BMW. At the trial the following September, defense attorneys portrayed Delon as a little lost boy who had fallen in with bad company. They also suggested that he had seen too many of his father's gangster films. Anthony got an eight-month suspended sentence.

Between his arrest and the trial, though, Delon had found a legitimate purpose, a fashion design business. Soon after his September trial, he presented his first collection of leather jackets at a promotional party.

Much as Delon cleaned up his act, first with the leather-jacket business and later with a foray into acting, he was still not suitable material for Stephanie. His previous flirtations, along with the court appearance, did not recommend him as a great marriage bet for any father's daughter, much less a rich and beautiful princess. Stephanie, just like her grandmother before who had befriended a jewel thief, seemed to be developing a proclivity for men with blemished pasts. In the mood for fun and adventure, she clearly saw Delon as a way of getting it.

Delon, according to close friends on both sides of the romance, tended to view his connection to Stephanie as a vehicle for career advancement. Nonetheless, he was also said to be extremely jealous of the affection and respect the prince conferred on his rival Paul Belmondo. Reflecting on the fact that Stephanie seemed to gravitate to sons of actors, one Parisian commented wryly: "If it doesn't work out with Delon, Stephanie could always try Nicolas Charrier [son of Brigitte Bardot] or even Christian Vadim [son of Roger]." Another friend of the couple maintained, "It was not a love affair, just a strong friendship. If it had been a real love affair, then it would have been hidden." Belmondo had tried, after all, to preserve some privacy in his relationship with the princess.

It seemed at first that this friend might have underestimated the persistence of the paparazzi who might be entirely to blame. But, as things would transpire, Delon's actions suggested otherwise. On one occasion, he leaked the details of their evening agenda to the press. To Stephanie, this was totally inappropriate and unacceptable. Their relationship, she decided, was finished. Stephanie promptly gave him the royal boot out of her life.

Princess Stephanie did not suffer any bouts of despair over Delon. Soon it was on to the next flirtation, this one with Stéphane Labelle, the son of a shoemaker. Though his background could not have been more different from that of her previous beaus, still Labelle was able to pass as an escort at numerous events. By then Stephanie was confident enough to also go places on her own. She turned up alone at a dinner party for Dior's Marc Bohan, her boss, and then spent much of the evening just observing other guests.

There were post-Delon suitors, who included François Hesnarlt, who later married Stephanie's best friend, Alix de la Comble; Christian de Beauvais, a count and working architect; and Swedish racing-car driver Stefan Johansson who finally decided Stephanie was "too fast for me"; and American-born actor Christopher Lambert, star of *Greystoke: The Legend of Tarazan, Lord of the Apes.*

The citizens of Monaco tended to adopt a forgiving attitude toward Stephanie's frenzied social life, according to a longtime confidante of Prince Rainier, because of the tragic loss of her mother. They also found themselves slightly amused by the young princess. As one government official put it, "She's as rambunctious as any kid her age. We're proud of her success and spirit."

Her next beau was Hollywood "Brat Pack" actor Rob Lowe, whom the princess met at the Deauville Film Festival. Soon after they would spend ten days together in Paris. Maybe it was his movie star charisma that some compared to that of Grace Kelly's leading man in *To Catch a Thief.* Film director Tony Richardson described Lowe's appeal thus: "I think he is the most talented young actor around. He has the sexuality and charm to become the next Cary Grant." Soon after their meeting they became inseparable, floating around Europe together, buying rings at Cartier in Paris. With Lowe's return to the States, they conducted the romance through transatlantic calls. Stephanie would soon turn up in California where she stayed for a time at Lowe's house there. Before their involvement, Rob and Stephanie dreamed about it. As Lowe recalls, "The princess and I discovered that we were both trying to meet each other for a real long time. But neither of us knew it." Except Joan Rivers to whom Lowe announced on the *Tonight* show, "Stephanie is my fantasy date."

"When we did meet," Lowe continues, "it turned out that she was going through the same thing as me. She'd go to sleep at night with a magazine with pictures of me by her bed at the palace." At one point, Lowe, unbeknownst to the princess, flew to Dallas because he had heard she would be at a dinner there. Stephanie was nowhere to be found. "I can't believe I went so far," Lowe says in retrospect. "All the way to Dallas just for a dinner."

Lowe remembers with affection the day they finally met in Deauville. "I was a wreck. I couldn't decide what to wear. I changed my clothes five times. I even took two showers. Finally I got dressed and did my hair. I don't do my hair—not ever—but for some strange reason I messed it up. Then I thought, this is ridiculous, so I got back in the shower and started again." Coming face-to-face with the princess proved to be as nerve-racking as the prelude to their meeting. "A woman, at last, had me in a panic," he admits. "I didn't know what to say so I picked up a potato chip and said, 'Pretty good, eh?' and she agreed, and we spent the next half hour on a potato-chip conversation. Finally, things worked out, and we got to talking on a much more personal level. It was unbelievable, like a dream come true, that I met her and two weeks later moved into her apartment."

Indeed, as one news magazine would observe, it was the sort of romance in the vein of Bianca and Mick Jagger, part soap opera, part Hollywood, played out in front of an international audience. Others would be watching as well. At Rainier's insistence, there was a bodyguard at Stephanie's side. On the one occasion the bodyguard was absent, Stephanie was allegedly accosted by a man and a woman outside the garage of her Paris apartment. As the story goes Stephanie was ordered at gunpoint to get back in the car, but keeping her wits about her she screamed and ran indoors. Under the threat of what looked then like an attempted kidnapping, Rainier became all the more convinced that Stephanie, with or without a boyfriend at her side, needed protection. Lowe had further to put up with an entourage including a press aide, hairdresser, and personal secretary to the princess. One of her palace entourage says, "Stephanie needs people to take care of her." Yves Roz, her record producer, goes even further. "Stephanie needs constant reassurance," he says. "She schemes to get love." Stephanie, trying to downplay the enormous press attention accorded this romance, insisted that they were only dinner companions. Reports of an engagement were vigorously denied. Whatever the nature of their relationship, it ended up with Lowe back in the arms of his former girlfriend, actress Melissa Gilbert, and the princess and the Hollywood heartthrob trading insults.

In reaction to headlines asking how Stephanie dumped Rob, the actor shot back with his own announcement. "She was with me," he declared, "for the publicity." Stephanie shrugged off the remark with, "He is a great friend and that is all." She added: "When he told the press how he conquered the princess, I pitied him. He used our friendship as a promotional tool." In truth, some of Stephanie's dates have been merely friendships. Jarel Portman, son of the celebrated architect and hotel mogul, was one of them. At the time of Stephanie's American launch of her swimwear collection, Portman flew from San Francisco to Atlanta to squire her around after a party at his parents' home there. Portman took the princess to a disco where they sipped champagne late into the night. They left holding hands, a gesture that might have been misinterpreted as something more than his good manners. "She hasn't been given a fair shake," Portman remarks. "It's hard to live the life of a princess." Squelching any potential rumors about a romance between them, Portman told reporters it would be geographically impractical.

The next romantic liaison would be far more intense and serious. But Stephanie paused long enough to tell London's *Daily Express:* "I have no desire to justify myself. For many boys I was the ultimate trophy. Many declared having an affair with me, but it was in their minds and nowhere else."

Stephanie defended herself against her critics, "People often accuse me of having an intense love life, but they don't really know what they are talking about. I don't run after men." Then, as if to emphasize her point, she added, "I'm not crazy about men in general. I've done nothing to make them pursue me." Such self-described indifference is in sharp contrast to her behavior, as described by her cousin Christian de Massy, who tells how Stephanie threw a bucket of ice on the head of a girl she thought was looking too much at her date in a nightclub.

Now, apparently contradicting her own words, Stephanie has come across the Atlantic for her new man. It would be an interesting reverse of fate. Whereas Grace left Hollywood for Monaco to marry Rainier, Stephanie has moved to Hollywood, where she is reported to be taking private acting classes, to live with her love. "I am now with the man I love and have no reason to hide it," Stephanie says. "I am proud to show our happiness to the world and to announce that we intend to be together for a long time." Only, this man would make Junot, once her father's chief nemesis, seem like a prince. His name is Mario Oliver Jutard, a French-born restaurant and nightclub owner, twelve years her senior. With his humble working-class background, the one-time waiter from Marseille was hardly the right sort of Romeo for Rainier's daughter.

Mario's lack of pedigree was not the only issue. There was the matter of his history with women—two quickie marriages and the accusations by another that he raped her. The princess remained undaunted by war stories that some of the women in his past told the newspapers. In 1982 Oliver came to the United States to help launch Guess jeans. His involvement was short-lived. While waiting to open his own club, he worked as a waiter at a restaurant, now closed, owned by Sonny Bono, an ex-husband of Cher. Mario married a stuntwoman, twenty-six-year-old Maria Kelly, whom he met at the restaurant. Their brief union, all of three weeks, ended in an annulment. "This man put me through hell," Kelly says. "He's a man with a shady past. I could blow him out of the water. But why bother. It will pass between him and Stephanie." From his former employer, Bono, came this analysis: "He's a good waiter, a great waiter. But it cracks me up that he's dating Stephanie. He's the last person . . . but that's Hollywood." That same year he was charged with raping a nineteen-year-old college student, Deana Nance. The rape charge was dropped and Mario pleaded no contest to a lesser charge of sexual battery. Nance told a London tabloid that she met Mario at a Bel Aire party, where they danced and talked until two in the morning. Then she proceeded to describe how he lured her into the bedroom, flung her on the bed, and with the help of a second man raped her.

"I live with this every day of my life," Nance says. "It is something I will never get over. If Princess Stephanie has any sense at all, she will dump this creep."

Mario strongly denied Nance's story and offered a different version in an interview reported in *People* magazine: "She was a girlfriend of a friend of mine. She got scared. Probably she didn't want him to find out I went out with her or something. We went out on Monday. The next Saturday she's having a good time in a nightclub, and they come to arrest me on Sunday. When we were together everything was fine." He adds: "I'm a very sensitive person. I wouldn't hurt anybody." It was during this stressful period that Mario married an Asian woman with two children. They stayed together for two years. Mario bailed out of that union because, he said, "I like to get out and meet people and go to clubs." Next there was another young woman, a nineteen-year-old model and prelaw student, Verna Richland. Apparently Mario liked her well enough to take her back home to France to meet his parents and to Paris, Rome, and Florence. Then Stephanie stepped into the picture. "Mario told me not to get jealous," she says. "That Stephanie was good P.R. for the club." She claims further that Mario cried in front of her many times and continued to call her. "He was always apologizing, always asking for another chance," she relates. "Everyone says he left me for Stephanie. But what she doesn't realize is that he left me for what she can do for him."

Tales of Mario's dubious past and current motives did nothing to temper Stephanie's passion. They met in the spring of 1986 through friends and then again, in October, at his fashionable Los Angeles nightclub, Vertigo. The place became a popular haunt of Brat Pack actors and other young trendies. Oliver prides himself on a certain exclusivity. In the West Coast disco culture, it is as difficult to gain entry to Vertigo as Harvard or Oxford. A princess, a familiar face at some of Europe's trendiest clubs, could lend panache to his place. Stephanie does not see things this way. "With Mario," she insists, "I know he is looking at me and not at a symbol."

According to the princess, it took just one look to bring them together. She describes their first meeting with great drama. "We were alone together in the restaurant linked by a gaze," she remembers fondly. "Around us people continued to dine without our taking any notice. It was like a flash. We didn't want to be separated again by planes and thousands of kilometers. I was so attracted to his smile and maturity. I discovered the security of having someone older at my side to help me and advise me and be a support in hard times." She credits Mario with giving her a greater sense of security about her work. "Before, I was a bit nervous professionally about America," she confesses, "and its reputation for devouring stars. But I'm not afraid anymore.

"I'm tired of not being appreciated for what I'm really worth," the princess adds, "I'm tired of hearing that my success is due to my birth certificate. I have the conqueror's rage in me and want to go and prove myself in the United States." Reflecting on her previous track record with men, she says, "The attitudes of the men in my past have made them temporary in my life. I always dreamed of a durable presence. Of course, I was only sixteen when I met Paul Belmondo. He was seventeen. We were very young and burnt out our love because we loved each other too much, too passionately. It's a pity for both of us that we shared this experience so young. If we'd met several years later, I'm sure things would have turned out differently. In the past four or five years I have grown up, learned more from life. Naturally I made mistakes in the past. Who doesn't? But with most people no one notices or cares. My mistakes were exposed to the public each time." Devoted as she may be to Mario, in a sense the princess's heart still belongs to Daddy. She returns to Monaco for royal duties. "It is around these obligations that I shall organize my life," she maintains. "I also hope to be much closer to my family, especially my father." On the subject of Mario, the princess says that she had spoken briefly about him to her father. "I suppose he [Rainier] is a bit apprehensive about it all—Mario, my career, my decision to leave for the States."

Possibly Stephanie has underestimated his concern. Newspaper reports placed the prince and the princess in the Caribbean island of Antigua for a fatherly chat last summer. There Rainier expressed his worries over her widely reported romance. The princess believes that, ultimately, her father will be happy with her choice. "That I've settled down," she explains. "That I'm with a man with whom I am having a stable relationship. That I'll no longer be drifting." At the same time, she points out that though her father might be a bit apprehensive about Mario's background, "He let my sister marry the man she wanted to so I don't see why I should be any different."

Mario's history does not seem to trouble her. "My past," Mario claims, "makes no difference to Stephanie." The princess bubbles: "Now it's not a teenager I'm in love with, but a man."

CHAPTER 8

Marriage and Motherhood

DIFFICULT moments lay ahead for Princess Caroline after her divorce. Just as she was establishing a life of her own, she suffered the devastating loss of her mother. Without a husband to cushion the blow or children to give her a sense of renewal, Caroline's inner strength was put to the test. The princess performed magnificently in this hour of tragedy. Caroline immediately took charge, handling the funeral arrangements, and more importantly, attending to her father's enormous grief. Later she assumed most of the First Lady duties that belonged to her mother. And fifteen months after Grace's death, the princess married a second time and over the next four years produced three children of her own.

The road back had not been easy. Following her 1980 divorce from playboy Philippe Junot, seventeen years older than the princess, Caroline was bereft. Like any newly divorced young woman, she had her share of romances, in her case enough to keep the paparazzi in business.

There was a love match in 1982 with the handsome and charming Argentine tennis star Guillermo Vilas, whom she accompanied to tournaments and on a romantic Hawaiian idyll. Vilas, a lover of the writings of Kahlil Gibran, sort of the Hindu version of Rod McKuen, even dedicated some of his own poems to the princess.

Despite the immortal words, their relationship proved to be short-lived and ended on a sour note. Caroline shared some of his literary ambitions. As a grade-school pupil, an essay she wrote about an animal was compared by a teacher to the style of Colette. With uncharacteristic modesty, the princess allowed, "Well, it was a pretty stupid teacher, but it really lifted my ego." In the period following her divorce and then the death of her mother, any boost to her self-confidence would do. The jottings in her diary revealed a somewhat deflated princess. "I do not think I am the ideal woman for a man," she wrote in her diary, "with my tormented past, my uncertain present, and perhaps my melancholy future." Caroline thought about writing a collection of short stories. She also busied herself with redecorating the ten-room apricot villa, a three-minute walk to the palace, that had been a wedding gift from her parents, and establishing her own Paris digs, a duplex in the chic seventh arrondissement. Onyx, her Alsatian guard dog, was a constant companion.

A few months before her death, Grace appraised Caroline's situation in a *People* interview. "Caroline hasn't had it easy," Grace said, "but she's adjusted very well. Having had two articles published recently, she would like to pursue her writing talent. She has a talent for it and writes equally well in French and English." By then, the princess had penned articles for British *Tatler* and *The International Herald Tribune.*

Caroline was linked more prominently with Robertino Rossellini, love child of Ingrid Bergman and Roberto Rossellini and a Monte Carlo real estate adviser. Marriage rumors flourished in the press, though there were other indications that they were really just friends. At one point, Robertino remarked, "Caroline is like a sister to me." No matter the nature of their involvement, he would prove a soothing presence after Grace's death.

The prince was fond of the young man, who was also a friend of Albert's as well. "Robertino likes Caroline a lot and she likes him a lot," Rainier said. "He is a faithful friend, discreet, solid, always present. Unhappiness has brought them together. For Caroline he is someone sure, in whom she can trust. It is a love that has lasted a long time." During this period, Robertino also experienced the loss of his own mother, the beloved and brilliant actress Ingrid Bergman, to cancer. Rainier even had Rossellini round to the family's enormous estate, Château de Marchais, about seventy-five miles north of Paris, for a weekend of riding and shooting pheasant.

The palace did little to cool rumors of an impending marriage between the two. Even Nadia Lacoste got in on the act, fueling the reports. "Since her divorce," Lacoste told the press, "Caroline has seen a lot more of Rossellini than anyone else. I cannot say this is the love of her life. Maybe one day it will be."

Robertino and Caroline skied in Zürs, Austria, in March of 1983. They also weekended in Rome. In May they were seen holding hands at the Grand Prix of Monaco Formula One auto race. But by summer the relationship had run its course, after Robertino was snapped by paparazzi in an affectionate pose with a starlet in a motorboat off the Greek isles in July. It was around this time that Caroline met Stefano Casiraghi, the man who would become her second husband. This was not, despite various reports, a rebound situation. "It was finished long before she met Casiraghi," Rossellini said. And Caroline herself acknowledged at one point, "Robertino was my opposite because he was always very calm." Later, while in Los Angeles, Caroline would tell reporters simply, "He [Rossellini] dropped me."

Was Caroline, who had tried so hard to forget the mistake of her first marriage, doomed to repeat it? Some friends and observers thought, judging from Casiraghi's reputation, this might be the case. For starters, he was, at twenty-three, three and a half years younger than Caroline, twenty-six going on twenty-seven. Among the Côte d'Azur crowd, Stefano had a reputation as a big spender who liked to lavish extravagant presents on his conquests.

A girlfriend of five years, twenty-four-year-old Pinuccia Macheda, whom he jilted for Caroline, said Stefano gave her a new Volkswagen Rabbit as a birthday present. Back in Milan Stefano might pick her up in the evening and ask if she would like to have dinner in Paris. "We would catch a plane, and a couple of hours later we'd be sitting in the latest 'in' restaurant ordering oysters and champagne." Stefano would later disappear from her life as precipitously. After Pinuccia Macheda's birthday party he told Macheda to meet him two weeks later at Porto Rotondo in Sardinia.

But during the voyage his yacht crossed paths with Caroline's off the coast of Corsica. Over the next five days they seemed to disappear together. Back on land they remained similarly close, tooling around in Caroline's Autobianchi and spending a great deal of time together in her Paris duplex apartment. In the fall the prince reluctantly had Casiraghi up to the château to do some pheasant-hunting. On December 9, the prospective groom turned up in the royal box at Monaco's annual International Circus Festival.

Ten days later, on December 19, the palace released a brief two-sentence statement: "His Serene Highness Prince Rainier of Monaco is happy to announce the marriage of Princess Caroline with Stefano Casiraghi. It will be celebrated Thursday, December 29, at the palace."

Whatever his private opinion of Stefano, the prince apparently gave his grudging stamp of approval to the union. Ten months earlier, in March of 1983, Rainier was asked by an interviewer whether Caroline should marry again. "I think it's indispensable," he said. "I don't think a young woman can be alone. I don't think it's right. And probably the second marriage would be a good one. The first one was a mistake."

Princess Grace had felt similarly. "Of course, I would like to see her married again one day, with children and a happy family life like I've had," Grace told a magazine. "But that is in the future."

Whether this union was what Grace had in mind for her daughter would remain a big question mark. Among other details, Caroline was reportedly three months pregnant at the time of her wedding. In this citadel of gambling, locals placed bets on her condition. Friends and observers wondered what her hurry was to get to the altar a second time. After all, it was the princess herself who vowed that once was enough. "People are always trying to remarry me," she had told *Elle* magazine in June of the previous year. "I don't want to remarry."

Rich, handsome, and athletic, if the strapping blond Casiraghi possessed any of Junot's playboy tendencies, it might be difficult for the princess to control his wanderlust. At the same time he shared the prince's obsession with money and would be enterprising and ambitious in the business arena.

"Junot at least had a terrific personality," a friend of the princess told one magazine. "Even Guillermo Vilas had a lot more to offer than Stefano. And you should see his friends—their conversations are pretentious and mostly about money." In contrast to the prince, who sometimes seems more like the king of the freebies, Stefano was quite free about spreading his money around. On top of staying for free at New York's Regency Hotel, owned by Loew's, which also owns a Monte Carlo hotel, according to one American tabloid, Rainier failed to tip the service staff. The Italian papers would also jump on Rainier after Stefano became a father. Apparently the prince banned the taking of pictures of Caroline and his third grandchild. Stefano, who had studied economics at Bocconi University, would start investing in all the boutiques and souvenir shops around the palace that the prince did not own.

"Casiraghi is a bloody doormat," Rainier's nephew, Christian de Massy declares. "Caroline was coming into that phase where she thought she should get serious. 'I need children. I need a man. I need children.' And they go on a boat, and she gets pregnant by Casiraghi. 'Why not marry the bugger and make kids and start her new life' . . . which she's done and *he* has become extremely rich in the process. That's the only reason I was kicking Junot's ass the other day. He could have become extremely wealthy, too, washing money, all the way to the Italian capital."

The official line was that Casiraghi was the son of a wealthy industrialist from Fino Mornasco, near Milan, who had oil interests, but was now more involved in real estate and construction. Stefano, according to spokesperson Lacoste, would be expanding interests in his father's business and would "step up his role exporting Italian shows and textiles to the United States."

Similar in origins to the bricklayer Kellys of Philadelphia, the Casiraghi family was also self-made. Stefano's grandfather had been a railroad gatekeeper, and his father, Giancarlo, made his fortune in Italy's post-World War II industrial expansion.

A Grimaldi-Casiraghi connection could prove even more expansionary. With Monaco only a half-hour drive from the French-Italian border, the principality would benefit from good relations with Italians who made the casino coffers larger and also invested in Monaco's development plans. In the future Stefano might prove a valuable ally of the principality.

Caroline and Stefano met, the palace line went, a year prior to their marriage. The setting, naturally, was a disco, Jimmy's in Monaco. They did one slow dance. But apparently that did not do it for Caroline, whose first husband, Junot, had captivated her immediately in another disco. But it was not until the following July that they sailed off into the sunset, literally.

"The woman can't choose her men," one Paris divorcée said. "No sensible divorcée, princess or otherwise, would marry someone that much younger, certainly not this quickly." Further, Caroline's first marriage had yet to get a papal annulment, which was supposed to be granted within the next year. Thus in the eyes of the Vatican, Princess Caroline was still Madame Junot. Her rumored pregnancy inspired a joke around the Paris jet-set: "Junot who the father is?" Said one insider, "He [Casiraghi] is fine for a flirt, for an affair, but not to marry when you are the Princess of Monaco." Among the Côte d'Azur crowd, Stefano was regarded as indolent, spoiled, and something of a playboy. "Stefano is a bit presumptuous," his ex-girlfriend Pinuccia asserted. "He thinks he can fool the whole world, but now I've opened my eyes. As far as his story with Caroline goes, it may well end up in a lot of silliness."

There was no pomp to the marriage ceremony, hardly a repeat performance of the first. Instead of an ornate church wedding, there was a fifteen-minute civil ceremony held in the palace's Chamber of Mirrors rather than in the Throne Room, the usual setting. With a hoped-for Vatican annulment still pending, Caroline could not marry in the church. Whereas prenuptial lunches and a ball for six hundred celebrities and royals marked her first wedding, the second time around there was, simply, a quiet buffet with twenty-three close friends and relatives. Caroline's engagement ring, made of three different sapphires, each a different color—pale blue, pink and yellow—was the only glittering detail.

Caroline dressed in Dior once again. Only this time the creation was not white, obviously, but a beige satin and crepe wraparound dress. She wore vestal-blue ribbons in her hair. The groom wore a conservative blue Valentino suit to their wedding.

In the months before her death Grace described the qualities she valued most in a potential son-in-law. "Character first," she said, "and someone who can provide for the girls, and look after them. Someone who is kind and has a sense of humor and is easy to get along with."

Some friends of Caroline's wondered aloud whether Stefano would have garnered Grace's approval. "He's a nice guy," one friend remarked, "but he's certainly not up to playing Prince Consort to Princess Caroline. God help him."

Hardly considered a witty raconteur, Stefano would appear quite ill at ease, if not altogether bored, at palace functions. "All he cares about are fast cars and fast boats," says one insider, "and buying into boutiques in Monaco so that if one day Caroline throws him out of her bed, it will be impossible to also throw him out of the principality—he'll own too much of it." Casiraghi even looked bored, one observer said, sitting at the same table as President Reagan at the Princess Grace Foundation benefit in Washington. He has been known to sit for two hours at social functions without saying one word.

Frequently Stefano would bow out on account of business. He would be traveling much of the time for his powerboat and construction firms, still other ventures of his. Caroline, as the palace was quick to point out at the time of her marriage, would continue to fill in as "First Lady" at official events. As such, it looked for a time like the couple led entirely separate lives.

Almost from the moment of Grace's death, Caroline took over. She would often fill in as the prince's escort. Deeply concerned about her father, who was filled with an immense grief, Caroline spent a great deal of time in her villa next to the palace to be close to and comfort him.

In the months prior to her second marriage, Caroline carried out the duties that had once been her mother's responsibility. Her first official function, following the mourning period, came in the last week of January 1983 at a "work and friendship" lunch at the Elysée Palace in Paris. There royalist Caroline managed to charm France's egalitarian Socialist President François Mitterrand. It was no small feat considering that Monaco's citizenry manage to duck

French taxes and the draft and by and large contribute virtually nothing to the Republic. Then in March, Caroline attended a Kennedy Center benefit in Washington, D.C., where Nancy Reagan narrated Ogden Nash's verses to Camille Saint-Saëns' "Carnival of the Animals," a program that Grace had been scheduled to do.

Back in Monaco that summer, Caroline accompanied her father to the annual Monaco Red Cross Ball, the high point of the principality's social season, on August 9. Later that month, the princess looked less regal in a Girl Scout's outfit as she and fifty-six others from the Monaco chapter, to which she had belonged as a child, set up a campsite on the sprawling seventeenth-century Grimaldi estate, the Château de Marchais, outside Paris.

Continuing the good works of her mother, Princess Caroline also served as president of the Princess Grace Foundation, the Monaco Garden Club, and the organizing committee for Monaco's annual Springtime Festival of International Arts. Additionally, Caroline kept in operation the hot line for Monaco's troubled teens that she founded two years before, in 1981. Above all, she was able to realize her mother's dream, the recreation of the Ballets de Monte Carlo. The princess talked Parliament into contributing monies for it. By then, the most resistant member had passed on, thus removing a major obstacle to achieving this goal.

It was at this time when Caroline was consumed by these duties, that Stefano entered her life, in July 1983. Just like her mother before her, Caroline would not let work keep her from having a family. Less than six months after her marriage, she gave birth to a son, Andrea Albert Casiraghi. Though weighing in at a healthy six pounds, ten ounces, he was noticeably premature. As such, the birth was largely unheralded.

The untitled infant would only be fourth in line of Monaco's succession. To date, however, his own father, Stefano, had not been given any of the fifty titles Prince Rainier might bestow upon him. Andrea Albert was named after both a friend of Casiraghi's who died of a pulmonary embolism a few years earlier and Caroline's brother. The same obstetrician who delivered Caroline, Albert, and Stephanie presided at this birth as well.

Like her mother, Caroline breast-fed her baby, who slept in the nursery next to her bedroom. Despite a small squadron of help, minus a nanny, Caroline stated her desire to care directly for her child. By the time the princess reached thirty years of age, she had given birth to two more children. What with the garden club, ballet, and other duties, it looked as if the princess might turn into a superwoman, juggling career and family. Reportedly spending every day, from 10:30 A.M. to 5 P.M., at her office in the palace, Caroline turned up late at one opening because, she apologized, "Andrea refused to eat his porridge." A daughter, Charlotte Marie Pomeline, named after Prince Rainier's mother, whom Caroline was often said to resemble in looks and personality, arrived on August 3, 1986; and then another son, Pierre, on September 5, 1987. The youngest Casiraghi, entering the world the same month that Grace had left it five years before, was a most welcome presence, bringing some joy at the time of this sad anniversary.

Caroline, like Grace, worried about spoiling the children. Her brood, however, are not royal since they are not the offspring of a reigning prince. Nor will they grow up believing, as did Caroline until starting school outside the palace at seven, that everyone has a name followed by "of Monaco." Caroline bathes her children and helps plan their menus. A devoted mother, she tries not to spend more than two days away from them. At six months, her firstborn, Andrea Albert, was along with his mother for a vacation in Key West, Florida, and at eight months on a skiing trip to St. Moritz.

The previous year, 1985, there had been some bumpy moments as well in the marriage. While he was away on business, Stefano was reported seen with various beauties. Then Caroline's old beau Robertino Rossellini turned up in Monaco to frolic with Caroline and her baby in a public pool. A few weeks later Caroline and Stefano reportedly went off on a second honeymoon in Sardinia. Rossellini faded from the scene, as did tales of Stefano and other women.

Caroline fretted, though, about Stefano's passion for boat racing. The danger of the sport was brought home to her after a racing friend of the couple's, Didier Pironi, was killed in waves off the Isle of Wight in mid-August of 1987. A week later, Caroline, heavily pregnant with Pierre, tried to dissuade Stefano from entering the Mumm Champagne Cowes Power Boat Classic on August 30. He participated anyhow, and came in fifth. Previously, Caroline watched from the palace window as her husband's boat blew an engine and disappeared from view in a cloud of black smoke during the first few minutes of the second annual Grand Prix Offshore Riccaronna Trophy, forcing him to drop out of the race.

On wheels, Stefano did not have much luck either. Earlier the same month that his boat went up in smoke, he entered the Atlas Rally, a cross-country auto race from Lyons, France, to Agadir, Morocco. The Subaru he was driving overturned in the southern Moroccan desert. He was pulled out by paparazzi who were tracking him.

"Stefano has read too many comic books," says a friend. "He gets behind the wheel of a fast boat or car and lives out his hero fantasies without really knowing what he's doing."

A lover of speed, Stefano has been clocked driving with his wife and infant daughter Charlotte at 170 kilometers. Caroline herself had a car crash in August of 1986 just two hundred yards from the spot where her mother had been killed four years previously. Driving alone in her Rolls-Royce from Monaco to the family's summer residence, Roc Agel, Caroline was blinded by the headlights of an approaching car and swerved into a parapet. Shaken, but not injured, she walked alone to a nearby house to seek help. The fender of her car was damaged.

Apparently marriage and children have slowed the couple's passion for adventure. Caroline's friends say she is calm, focused, and in charge of her life. Stefano, one friend explains, has been good for her. "Stefano is young, but very mature," the friend says. "He has a lot of the qualities her mother had. He is disciplined, devoted, reserved, warm. In him she has found her mother."

Stefano as well holds himself in high esteem. Prior to his marriage to the princess, he told *Gente*, the right-wing Italian weekly: "Although I'm twenty-three, I have the mentality and experience of a man of thirty. I'm a born businessman . . . I'm involved in business in all sectors, from exporting footwear to building and investment."

Already Stefano has invested royally in Monaco. He has bought into two Dior boutiques as well as purchased a Ford franchise that he plans to use to sell fancy cars. Clearly, Stefano is demonstrating the same financial finesse as his father-in-law. As head of state, Rainier's royal compensation is about $4.6 million a year. It comes from revenues from taxes on tourism and local light industry. Through wise investments he has vastly increased the family fortune. Each member of the family receives a generous allowance. An example of his largesse was the lavish yacht Rainier was reported to have presented to Caroline as a surprise when Charlotte was born. Asked what he liked about Caroline's family prior to their marriage, Stefano told *Gente,* "They're healthy people, not spoiled and vicious like most aristocrats."

With Stefano quite the up-and-coming businessman, and Caroline dashing here and there to meetings while attending to their three children, this two-career couple clearly has higher ambitions. Whether a promotion to "First Family of Monaco" is in the offing depends on whether Caroline's brother Albert can find a suitable bride.

CHAPTER 9

What Next?

"**I** could have beaten her like a gong without making her give way. But you wait and see, Stephanie is going to be the most interesting of my children."

Those words, spoken twelve years ago by the late Princess Grace of Monaco in a private conversation at the Grimaldi holiday home, could not have been more prescient. In the five years since her mother's death, Stephanie has launched three successful careers, as a model, swimsuit designer, and pop star. Pursuing these goals has been one way for her to move past her grief.

Caroline, on the other hand, immediately took over Princess Grace's First Lady duties and also added wife and mother to her list of titles. Caroline is dutiful while Stephanie is daring. Though their goals are completely different, they are wary of each other. Stephanie, once terrified of her older sister's tongue-lashings, has broken out from under her yoke. The timing could not be worse. Palace watchers say that Caroline, positioning herself to overtake Albert as successor to their father, views Stephanie's impulsive behavior as a threat to the royal image. "Stephanie is standing on her own legs and saying to her sister, 'Go back to your flowerpot hats,'" says cousin Christian de Massy. "Caroline is discovering that Stephanie is becoming a liability and a disgrace to the family."

In an interview with *Life* magazine a few months after Grace's death, Rainier allowed, "They [the two princesses] are fond of each other, but perhaps Caroline, for the moment, is too much of the big sister and Stephanie resents her authority a little bit."

Their rivalry seems to go all the way back to childhood. All kinds of expectations are tied to the love given the oldest child, while the youngest is adored without experiencing the same pressure. Royals are clearly not immune to such family configurations. Stephanie's business achievements now make Caroline's accomplishments pale by comparison. In order to ensure her supremacy, Caroline must invest her own duties with the utmost importance. This may involve reining in her younger sister. In the case of Caroline, a divorcée, it may also be a form of atonement for her own mistakes in the past. Ironically, just as Philippe Junot represented for Caroline independence from her parents, Stephanie's Mr. Wrong, Mario Oliver, has enabled her to rebel similarly against Caroline.

So what does the future hold for Stephanie, whose hair has gone from red to green in a couple of hours, who wears three earrings in one ear but insists that she does not dress to shock? "I don't look like this to be rebellious," she says. Even so, Stephanie managed to make Blackwell's 1986 list of the world's worst-dressed women, a title that apparently caused her no shame or discomfort.

What is certain is that this young princess will always be an individualist, believing, above all else, in feeling comfortable with herself. Her message to teenagers: "Stand out in the crowd rather than follow it." Stephanie says of her own appearance: "I don't like wearing makeup, just a little eyeliner and lipstick. I adore jeans and cowboy boots."

Nowadays Stephanie spends most of her time in America enjoying the companionship of Mario Oliver. Around Los Angeles, home to so many movie stars that nobody makes much of a fuss about celebrities, there is no royal treatment for the princess, a circumstance that pleases her. Indeed, at a West Los Angeles sports club, where the princess does her push-ups, she seems no different to other members there. A *Los Angeles Times* reporter recently observed that with a deep tan, white teeth, trim physique, and healthy glow, Stephanie looks much the same as any other member. What's more, as she sits around the club, Stephanie seems to be at perfect ease with herself. No one asks for her autograph and, unlike in Europe, the paparazzi leave her alone. She has even asked the club management not to put princess on her membership card.

In her own words, Stephanie says, "I think I blend in really well here. People come up and talk to me. I live a normal life. I don't live the life of a star. I'm just a normal person made of flesh and blood like everyone else."

On her life with Oliver, the princess says that they live in a small rented house with a pool and three puppies. "Our favorite thing to do is just lie back in the sun and see friends and be settled like normal people." She adds: "We have our really close friends and that's it. We don't see other people. And, besides, Mario sees enough people at Vertigo. He's a very sociable person—he has to be in his business. I don't want to be in the jet-set."

Oliver only goes to the club weekends. Otherwise he works at home. Since opening in 1985, Vertigo has become one of the hottest clubs in America. Now there are plans to open in Paris, Tenerife, Buenos Aires, and Toronto. "We'll be like Régine's," he says. The princess, however, is no longer the disco queen that she once was. "I like the club," she says, "but there is really no point to my going there. I come there for him. I don't come there just to sit around and look stupid. So I have dinner there once in a while with him and then I just leave."

Like the locals, Stephanie makes career plans by the pool. She is not content to just sunbathe. Previously, she enjoyed success in modeling, fashion, and pop music. Like Caroline, she has also had an article published. But her interview with rock star Rod Stewart made headlines in over fifteen countries. In France *Elle* bought the article and, after seeing the photographs that accompanied it, made it a cover story. With these accomplishments on hold, she contemplates a film career and another record.

The princess plans to do more interviews with rock stars. Music continues to be one of her major interests. However, Stephanie clearly prefers to be center-stage herself. Now under the management of Joe Ruffalo, who also represents Prince, she hopes to follow in her mother's footsteps and go into films. But she remains cautious in this area. "I have to be very careful because of my family and my own image," she explains. "I'm not going to take just any film script. I've already been offered about fifty, and they're all dreadful."

Her fascination with show business began in childhood at her mother's side. "I used to love my mom to tell me stories about Hollywood," she says. There were rumors that Stephanie would appear in a guest spot on *Dynasty* following the Grimaldi family's November 1985 visit to the set. To date she has yet to hobnob with the Carringtons. Stephanie also auditioned for the part of Maggie in a production of *Cat on a Hot Tin Roof,* but did not get it.

The princess says, however, that she is more confident than ever. "I used to be really shy," she says. "When I'd have to greet friends of the family, I'd be blushing. It's growing up and getting out that has made the difference. I am sure that modeling helped me a lot even just in look and attitude. But I'm still shy."

Her growing confidence has allowed Stephanie to defend herself against critics. "People have always said a lot of trash about me," she claims. "Maybe I had something to prove. That I could work on something and have it recognized by the profession. That I wasn't just a tomboy."

In response to questions about drugs, the princess says, "If I did drugs, then how could I do all the things I do and keep going?" Her healthy glow would indicate that she is leading a wholesome existence.

Much as she despairs about her princess role, no one can take that away from her. Occasionally she will use her royal prerogative. Once when she was intending to fly from Paris to Nice, she discovered the plane was full. Stephanie informed the check-in staff of her status and then promptly threw a temper tantrum. She got on the flight.

She tends to be more egalitarian, if not outright generous with friends. As a result, she seems to have more friends than she can count. Once she picked up the tab for ten people along on a vacation in the island of Mauritius. "I am not fooled," she says. "I am not taken in. But I do need it right now. At least I know I need it. But one day I'll tell them the party's over. I will know when to quit."

For the moment Stephanie is clearly enjoying life even if that does put her over budget sometimes. "It's terrible to find your bank accounts in the red," she says, "and that happens to me so often. I buy on impulse. I make most of my payments by credit card. And that's extremely dangerous. I'm a terrible spendthrift. And my bankers always complain about this. They tell me I ought to invest, but I regard money as pieces of paper which I hand over in exchange for something else." Her mother, by contrast, was far more conservative about money. Grace allegedly never threw anything away, would sometimes give people a two-year-old box of chocolates, and wore the same maternity dresses for both Caroline and Albert. Caroline, a pal of Dior's Marc Bohan, reportedly gets free dresses, and now husband Stefano has a financial interest in two Dior boutiques.

Stephanie longs for privacy, one of the few things she could never pay for by credit card. "All the publicity they put around me," she says, "is the most difficult thing to come to terms with." Uppermost in her mind is to find the happiness that seems to have eluded her since the tragic death of her mother. Possibly this may mean settling down and having children. "I love children," she says, "and I hope to have them soon so they'll have young parents."

Then, in a rare admission, she adds, "Sometimes I envy my sister and wish I was going home to a husband and children. I even walk past shops selling tiny shoes and want to put them on a baby's feet. But usually because I love my job and everything that goes with it, I am glad to be who I am. I like the atmosphere of show business."

At the same time she harbors a fantasy about a normal home life: "I am preparing breakfast myself for the man I love. A homey couple living in Los Angeles with plenty of dogs around in a sun-drenched house open to our friends." She goes on: "I really am very romantic. Sometimes I need a gentle, silent presence and the warmth that comes from being with someone you love."

The question remains whether Prince Rainier will allow Stephanie to marry the man of her dreams, "He let my sister," she says, "so I don't see why he wouldn't let me." Of course, Mario's history does not recommend him as the perfect son-in-law, even for someone who is not a princess. "I am sorry for the tabloids," Stephanie vows, "but there will be no more scandals around me."

In a sense her heart may still belong to Daddy, who all too frequently doted on his not-so-dutiful daughter. "Monaco is magic," she says. "It seems more beautiful every time I go there. My father is all alone so I go there a lot to be with him because he has nobody now."

Her loyalty to Monaco remains. "I love my country," she says, "and I take my duties very seriously. I'll always be by my father in everything he does."

Among the family there is concern about Stephanie despite her glowing descriptions of life in Los Angeles. The intensity that she has brought to her professional accomplishments, those close to her say, may be her undoing in her private life. "She does have a streak of masochism in her," a relative says. "She lives so intensely. Being timid as well is a problem. Very often the timid also go overboard." There is an almost hysterical quality to Stephanie, who laughs at most anything. She also gnaws at her nails.

Stephanie clearly wants to get on with her own

work and eventually a family of her own. She will leave the power struggle to her brother and sister. Back at the palace there is a battle royal over who will rule this fairy-tale principality. At a dinner in Paris, Stephanie, after a scolding from Caroline, who also turned up there, was overheard telling a friend, "Ma *soeur*—you know, my sister—she really does take herself for a princess."

Indeed, if Caroline's Monaco activities are any indication, then she is proving herself to be a more suitable candidate to take over the tiny principality. Though Albert apprentices behind the scenes at fiscal and governmental meetings, Caroline has a far more powerful public image.

As First Lady she has taken on all her mother's duties. "First Lady," she demurs. "It's a big word. I work for my country as everyone else here works. If I can do something in an area I know a little bit about, that's very well. In the end it is a job like any other." It is also a job that could be taken away from her at any time should Albert find a suitable wife. As one family member puts it, "She won't like it at all. Caroline, married twice and the mother of three children, will be finished. After all, who thinks about Princess Anne since Princess Di." He continues, "If Albert marries a woman with two centimeters of character, after six months his new wife will say, 'Get her [Caroline] out of the palace.' Caroline will be left with vitally critical decisions like 'Ah, what color should we paint the opera house or where do we put the new public latrines."

With a husband and three children behind her, Caroline has a ready-made royal family in a country dependent on heirs as insurance against taxes and a military draft. Further, because of the job Grace did for Monaco, putting it on the map, the duties of First Lady hold enormous sway with the citizenry there. Caroline, extremely visible in this role, is building a constituency for herself. Caroline, for example, runs Monaco's Princess Grace Foundation while Albert heads up its American arm.

Whereas Caroline is headstrong, Albert is somewhat retiring. Friends say that if Albert has one fault, it may be that he is "too nice." Monégasques are used to strong leaders. Albert has yet to assert himself with his own father. The irony of his situation, it seems, is that his carefully planned path to power has been mapped out by his father, at whose side he sits in the Council of Ministers. "I think Albert is in a bit of a difficult situation," says one observer. "If the prince were not around, then Albert could develop his own character. He can't exactly be himself now." The prince's public statement some years back about abdicating as soon as his son is ready to rule may have inhibited Albert further. At twenty-three, Rainier took power; Albert is almost thirty and yet to step into his father's role with the same flamboyance and zeal Caroline brings to her mother's duties.

On paper Albert looks better than his sister. He has a degree in political science from Amherst College in America. After graduation he spent six months as an ensign aboard the French naval ship *La Jeanne d'Arc,* and then later studied international finance in New York before returning to Monaco for more leadership lessons from his father. The death of his mother, it was thought by many, would make him tougher. Still, his essentially shy and gentle nature would be no match for Caroline's volcanic Mediterranean personality.

Albert, caught between his bombshell sisters, has

yet to find a wife. Considered by many the world's most eligible bachelor, he likes to play the field and vowed not to marry before he was thirty. Belgian-born author/actress Monique von Vooren, old enough to be Albert's mother, remembers meeting him at a party six years ago in New York. "I remember Albert asked me to dance," she recalls, "and he danced with me the whole evening. Being a generation older, I was nonplussed and flattered. He certainly had his pick of any young attractive girl in the room. But he picked on me and did not stop dancing with me the whole night, and then he wanted to know what I was doing the next night. I told him it was not possible to go out." Albert is apparently in no hurry to continue the dynasty; his most suitable relationship to date was with Catherine Oxenberg, Hollywood actress and cousin of the last king of Yugoslavia.

"If the prince were going to die soon and knew it," a relative says, "he'd go to his daughter who is not making any more problems, who is married and has two sons. If he went to the Monégasques, they would tell him, 'Ah, she's doing a good job.'"

Nothing in Monaco's Constitution makes it illegal for Rainier to say his first daughter shall rule Monaco, though the Grimaldis have always followed the line of the oldest male. Rainier himself had to fight off the ambitions of his older sister, Princess Antoinette.

"Caroline may have to take over," family friend Vera Maxwell predicts. "I think Rainier's having a difficult time getting Albert away from his sailing and being out with people. Albert hasn't found a girl yet who is suitable to be Princess of Monaco. Caroline is just a charming woman. She is a great wife and mother and a great asset to the principality."

Caroline, by all accounts, is taking the royalty business the most seriously. "Albert is a nice guy who happens to be prince," a relative explains. "He would be happy as an executive in a company. He doesn't take himself too seriously." Stephanie, creative and explosive, where Caroline is organized and subtle, would be successful at any creative endeavor. "Princess or not," people say, "by her own right she is someone who has character, albeit maybe a bit too much." If Caroline were not a princess, however, in the words of Christian de Massy, "she would probably be doing research in child psychology, which she studied, or spraying perfume—Chanel No. 5—on somebody in Bloomingdale's."

Should Rainier find it too painful to choose between Caroline and Albert, *première dame* and perennial bachelor, then perhaps Stephanie would get star billing. Maybe the princess would give up Mario for Monaco.

If Stephanie ruled Monaco, what would it be like? One can only imagine! The national anthem would be a Bruce Springsteen number. Swimsuits would be a major national industry. All Monégasques born on the same day as Stephanie would get a complimentary holiday in Mauritius. Levi 501's would be the school uniform. The new form of salute would be a casual wave. Instead of the Monte Carlo Orchestra performing in the palace courtyard, Michael Jackson would appear in concert. Atmo, her German shepherd, would be second-in-command. Rainier and Albert would be accorded every comfort inside the palace; Caroline would be assigned to Nicaragua as Monaco's first consul there. Being boring would be punishable by law.

Whatever the outcome, Princess Grace would

have been very proud of both her daughters: Caroline assuming the responsibilities, for however long, of First Lady of Monaco as well as marriage and motherhood; and Stephanie stretching her creative talents, just like Grace Kelly, to stardom.

CHAPTER 10

The Press and the Princesses

SOMETIMES their lives have seemed more soap opera than high society, more rock star than regal, and on occasion, even more distasteful than distinguished. Small wonder, then, that the international press coverage of the two Princesses of Monaco has been so relentless over the years. Still, with no power beyond their tiny principality, why are they the focus of so much attention? Apart from attending to a few official duties, namely balls and charity events, the princesses lead lives quite similar to other jet-setters and aristocrats. Why, then, has there been so much interest in them?

"In every democratic nation," says Ray Browne, a professor of popular culture and English at Bowling Green University in Ohio, "there is always a demand for something bigger and stronger. And royalty provides that." Monaco's popularity, he adds, has much to do with the type of family they are. "The Windsors are just dull people who don't know how to enjoy themselves." Browne explains. "Latins like the Grimaldis are spacey and enjoy life." Browne continues: "Even though most people respect the Windsors, gamblers and fast-livers like the Grimaldis more. They wish they could live in Monte Carlo with casinos and fast cars. The Grimaldis represent excitement and danger."

Cindy Adams, a syndicated columnist and newscaster, echoes his thinking. "America has always gone dotty over anyone with a title," she claims, "even if they have one eye, one leg, or they're gay. Our society is starting to become made up of the person who is out on bail and all other sorts of low-life. People we don't know, we revere. The Grimaldis are popular because they have fallen off their pedestals. We don't see them as untouchables. Especially Stephanie, who is one of us."

People magazine senior editor Carol Wallace, who specializes in royalty, attributes the popularity of Caroline and Stephanie to Princess Grace: "I think in their particular case you have to take a look at who their mother was, and now there is a curiosity with the kids. The girls would not have caused a blip on the interest meter if they had been the daughters of the King of Spain." The daughters' beauty and jet-set lives, she adds, fascinate the public. "Unlike Princess Diana," Wallace explains, "both Stephanie and Caroline had led worldly lives by a young age, and have had far more freedom. The Grimaldi girls got away with a lot more."

Another reason for all the media attention may be the hard-to-get posture of the princesses, making them even more alluring. And the competition gets hotter to score the interview. At the same time, palace press officer Nadia Lacoste entices with tidbits of information, enough to keep up the interest, but never really delivering much of anything. Either inspired or irritated, the tabloid press resorts to rumors.

With more savory practitioners of journalism, Lacoste may hold out the promise of an interview, often with absolutely no intention of granting it. Or she may just sabotage it altogether. Case in point: this book. The Princess Grace Hospital in London sent us a letter praising Caroline's good deeds and enclosing pictures of her looking quite sweet and caring with children and the elderly there. Over a month later, after we rang up Lacoste and sent off a letter regarding interviews with the princesses, we heard from the hospital out of the blue. They were very worried. They had been told by the palace that if they spoke to us, any support would be cut off. Needless to say, they were as baffled as we were about why the palace would object to their giving information that could only reflect positively on Princess Caroline. All too often, it seems, frivolous or unflattering details get printed instead.

Syndicated *New York Daily News* columnist Liz Smith does not attribute the popularity of the princesses to their titles, but instead to the fact that people are interested in what they are told they need to be. "They aren't real royalty," she says, "but a minor ruling family. In times of world depression, they provide the press and the public with a good diversion."

Indeed, with their romantic and raunchy lifestyles, the Grimaldi princesses have provided lively diversions from a world burdened by such pedestrian matters as how to make the rent money and put food on the table. As far as their futures are concerned, as the world economy worsens, their stock as glitzy celebrities increases. With weighty international issues like nuclear disarmament, South African apartheid, and the possible collapse of the global stock market prominent in the news, the power struggle between Caroline and Albert will provide a throwback to childhood skirmishes and offer the public a mini-Greek drama, really a royal playlet. Younger sister Stephanie, with her shocking behavior, will continue to offer her own dramas, including her upcoming autobiography that features the men in her life. So far Princess Stephanie is making notes, with different-colored pencils. No matter what shade she chooses, the future of both Stephanie and her older sister Caroline promises to be bright.

About the Authors

SUSAN CRIMP is a journalist and the author of two books, *Ice Sports* and *Careers in Radio and Television*. She previously worked for Capital Radio of London. She now makes her home in New York City.

PATRICIA BURSTEIN is a journalist and author of two books, *Farrah* and *Family Holiday*, a novel. A former *People* magazine assistant editor, she is now a freelance writer living in New York City. Her articles have appeared in various magazines, including *New York, Savvy,* and *Harper's Bazaar.*

THE BRIGHTEST STARS...

MERYL STREEP: RELUCTANT SUPERSTAR by Diana Maychick

The first biography of this dazzling, articulate film star. With 8 pages of photos.

_____ 90246-8 $3.50 U.S.   _____ 90248-4 $4.50 Can.

ROBERT DE NIRO: THE HERO BEHIND THE MASKS by Keith McKay

A revealing look at one of today's most brilliant actors. Includes 16 pages of photos.

_____ 90475-4 $3.95 U.S.   _____ 90476-2 $4.95 Can.

ROBERT DUVALL: HOLLYWOOD MAVERICK by Judith Slawson

Leading the new breed of Hollywood hero. With 8 pages of dramatic photos.

_____ 90422-3 $3.95 U.S.   _____ 90423-1 $4.95 Can.

KATHLEEN TURNER by Rebecca Stefoff

The first biography of Hollywood's newest, sexy—and very daring—superstar. With 8 pages of glorious photos.

_____ 90604-8 $3.50 U.S.   _____ 90605-6 $4.50 Can.